THE HISTORY & [WESTMINSTER ABBEY]

BY LAWRENCE E. TANNER, M.V.O., V.P.S.A.

THE HISTORY & TREASURES OF
WESTMINSTER ABBEY

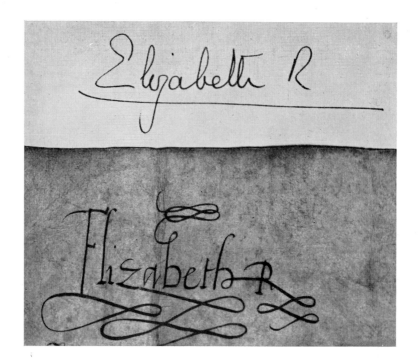

A ROYAL PECULIAR

It is appropriate that the opening of this book should carry the signatures of the two Queens Elizabeth, for the first founded the present Collegiate Church of St. Peter in Westminster, and the second, our Sovereign Lady, is its "Visitor".

In ecclesiastical terms Westminster Abbey is a "Royal Peculiar," which means that the Dean and Chapter are an independent body owing allegiance to no diocese, recognising the authority of the Visitor only. Thus the Abbey belongs to neither section nor group; it belongs to all who share the mother tongue and our reverence for the Christian creed. In this ancient church much of our history has been enacted; it stands for our ideals and our beliefs, and for over a thousand years the men of our race have given to it their art, their skill, their devotion and their wealth.

This book is published as the 38th Sovereign since the Norman Conquest comes to Westminster for her hallowing. It is published, also, at a time when the Abbey is in very great need, for the years have taken their toll of the fabric.

There are still men able and willing to give their art, their skill and their devotion—to make the repairs now so urgent—but more must give *something* of their wealth. Our forbears gave us this wonderful heritage, that we might today enjoy its peace and its beauty; we, in our turn, must ensure that those who follow us can enjoy them too.

First Impression 1953
MADE AND PRINTED IN GREAT BRITAIN AT BECCLES, SUFFOLK, BY WILLIAM CLOWES & SONS, LTD
FOR THE PUBLISHERS, PITKIN PICTORIALS, LTD, 9 NORTHINGTON STREET, LONDON, W.C.1

Her Majesty the Queen, Visitor of the Collegiate Church of St. Peter in Westminster. Her Majesty wearing the Imperial State Crown is arrayed in the Purple Robe of State and bears the Sceptre with the Cross and the Orb. The Armills were the gift of the Governments of the Commonwealth countries on the occasion of the Coronation. This portrait, taken by Cecil Beaton, was commanded by Her Majesty for this book. The decor symbolises Westminster Abbey.

This picture of the Procession leaving the Abbey after an Installation of Knights of the Bath was specially painted in 1747 by Canaletto for Dr. Joseph Wilcocks, the then Dean of Westminster. The Knights in their robes are followed by the Officers of the Order. Then comes the Dean of Westminster in his mantle as Dean of the Order, immediately preceding the Great Master. In the background, in the porch of the West Door, can be seen the Royal Cook with his cleaver ready to strike off the spurs of unworthy knights. Dean Wilcocks added the Western Towers to the Abbey, and it was partly to show these towers which had just been completed, greatly to the Dean's satisfaction, that the painting was commissioned. It was bequeathed to the Dean and Chapter by the son of Dean Wilcocks in 1792, and has hung in the Deanery ever since. Canaletto, an Italian, came to London in 1746 and during his stay of two years painted many of his striking architectural studies. He was a master of intricate and authentic detail as this painting so clearly illustrates. His works are very valuable and are eagerly sought by collectors; this one can justly be termed an "Abbey Treasure."

THE HISTORY AND TREASURES OF
WESTMINSTER ABBEY

by

LAWRENCE E. TANNER, M.V.O., V.P.S.A.
Keeper of the Muniments and Library

WITH A FOREWORD BY
THE VERY REV. ALAN C. DON, K.C.V.O., D.D.
Dean of Westminster

PITKIN · LONDON

THE GREAT APSE at the east end of the Abbey is one of the most striking features of Henry III's church. Its lofty proportions are accentuated by its narrowness; its grace affords an admirable setting for the High Altar and the Shrine of St. Edward. The High Altar, where the principal Abbey services are celebrated, stands against an ornate reredos screen remodelled in 1867 after Sir Gilbert Scott's designs. The back of this screen is of 15th-century date. The Sanctuary is flanked by medieval tombs and sedilia, and partly hung with tapestry. To the left is a fine hexagonal pulpit of the 17th century with a wooden sounding board.

CONTENTS

With 80 exclusive photographs by Harold White, F.I.B.P., F.R.P.S., 50 studies of detail by R. P. Howgrave-Graham, F.S.A., Assistant Keeper of the Muniments, Westminster Abbey, and more than 40 other illustrations.

The simple majesty of the entrance to Henry VII's Chapel.   A study made by Harold White shortly after dawn.

FOREWORD BY THE DEAN OF WESTMINSTER

OF books about Westminster Abbey there is no end; for, indeed, the subject is inexhaustible. As a Christian church where worship has been offered daily for nine hundred years; as a place of pilgrimage where the body of St. Edward, King and Confessor, still rests within the Shrine behind the High Altar, and where, in the Nave, the grave of the Unknown Warrior commemorates the great host who, nine centuries later, laid down their lives in two world wars; as the scene of successive Coronations since 1066; as the burial place of Kings and Queens, and the last resting place of men and women famed in the history of our race; as a supreme example of the glory of medieval architecture, and a treasure house of the art of sculptors and craftsmen of many generations; as a home of church music, and as a "Royal Peculiar" which, belonging to no diocese, belongs to all, Westminster Abbey has acquired a unique place in the estimation of the English-speaking peoples all the world over.

No single author and no one book could deal with every aspect of so many sided a subject; a whole library of books exists already and others will yet be written because the fascination of the Abbey never fades, and those over whom it casts its spell will ever seek to probe and share the secret of its manifold appeal.

The author of this book has many qualifications for his task, and, not least, the happy gift of combining wealth of knowledge with a clear style. He traces the history of the Abbey with the sure touch of a scholar who has devoted many years of his life to the study of his subject. As Keeper of the Muniments, Mr. Tanner has had access to a collection of documents that surpasses in range and interest that of any other great church in this country. The fruits of his research have been

The Very Reverend Alan C. Don, K.C.V.O., D.D.

★　　★　　★

skilfully used to enrich and enliven his narrative, and the result is a book which will be read with pleasure and profit by all who wish to learn something of the story of the Collegiate Church of St. Peter in Westminster, commonly called The Abbey.

I count it an honour to have been invited by the publishers to write a short foreword. In return I would congratulate them on the choice and quality of the illustrations that adorn the text. In this Coronation year, and for years to come, the book is assured of a ready welcome.

April 1953　　　　　　　　　　*Alan C. Don*

This unusual view of the Nave and the Western Towers is to be obtained from Dean's Yard. On this side of the Church were situated the conventual buildings of the Abbey, many of which remain. The Chapter House, Dormitory, Cloister, Infirmary, Abbot's Lodgings, Refectory and Guest House are to be seen today. But here once stood other buildings; a farm, a great granary to satisfy the daily requirements of the kitchen, and the almonry where alms and charity were disbursed daily by the monks.

The portion of the Bayeux Tapestry reproduced below depicts the Abbey as it was in the mid-11th century. Though crude it corroborates the few facts known of King Edward's church; its romanesque arches, the great crossing with its lantern and the eastern apse. The funeral procession of the dead King approaches St. Peter's Church. His open bier is escorted by a prelate with a crozier, and monks with books and bell ringers. To indicate that the building was a new one, a man is shown fixing the weathercock.

I

THE NORMAN BEGINNINGS

THE first Church at Westminster is said to have been built early in the 7th century during the later years of Ethelbert, King of Kent (d. 616) and shortly after the coming of St. Augustine to England. If this was so it would probably have been built with re-used Roman bricks, and have been rectangular in shape with a rounded chancel at its eastern end. No trace, however, has ever been found of it, although it is believed to have stood a little to the west of the present Church and to have extended eastwards under the present Nave. Later legend asserted that it had been miraculously consecrated by St. Peter himself, and that he had promised to take both it and the island in the Thames—Thorney Island—on which it stood under his special protection.

It is certain, however, that in the succeeding centuries there was a monastic establishment on the spot, and there is a further tradition that in the 10th century St. Dunstan found it in decay and brought monks from Glastonbury to infuse new life into it. It is with the accession of Edward the Confessor in 1042 that history takes the place of legend and tradition. He is the real founder of Westminster, and it was due to his devotion to St. Peter that he determined to renew and improve the earlier Church which had suffered from the incursions of the Danes and was almost in ruins. It is possible that there was already a palace in close proximity to the Church, but however that may be Edward made Westminster his principal residence, and the rebuilding of the Church became the chief interest of his later years. The new Church was far more ambitious than its predecessor. It introduced the Norman Romanesque style of architecture into England, and although it followed in plan the churches of Normandy of the period in its general dimensions it far exceeded in size any 11th-century Norman church which has survived. No trace of the Confessor's Church now remains above ground, but considerable foundations exist under the floor of the present Nave and elsewhere. From these it was possible to construct a ground plan of the Church. It was found that it had had an internal length of 322 feet and consisted of an apsidal choir of two bays, transepts, and nave of twelve bays. There were also the foundations of two western towers, although it is possible that these were a slightly later addition. It may be for this reason that they do not appear, for what that may be worth, in the almost contemporary representation of the Church in the Bayeux Tapestry. Except that the transepts were shorter the ground plan almost exactly coincided with that of the existing Church.

Edward the Confessor lived just long enough to see his new Church consecrated, but a few days later he died and was laid to rest within its walls. He had lavishly endowed the Monastery with lands in many counties, and with some of these, as, for instance, the Oxfordshire village of Islip where he himself had been born, the connection is maintained at the present day. These lands were confirmed to the Monastery by William the Conqueror and his successors, who were anxious to establish themselves as the lawful successors to the Confessor. It was for this reason that the Conqueror took the momentous decision to be crowned in the Abbey Church with which the name of the Confessor was in future to be inseparably connected. His example was followed by his successors, and thereby a precedent was set which has been followed to the present day. As the Coronation Church, and under the fostering care and protection of the Norman dynasty, Westminster began to assume an importance among the Benedictine Monasteries which it had not previously possessed. This was still further increased by the growing veneration in which the memory of the Confessor was held. He had always been beloved in his lifetime by his subjects for his simple piety, and in their memory a golden radiance seemed to blur the ineffectiveness of his reign when contrasted with the brutal efficiency of the Norman conquerors. It was almost inevitable in that age that before long legends and miraculous happenings should gather round the Confessor's tomb.

Men told, for instance, how William and Archbishop Lanfranc, at a council held within the Westminster precincts, had wished to deprive the last of the Saxon bishops, Wulstan of Worcester, of his See. But the old man had risen with dignity and had said that although he was well aware of his own unworthiness he would only resign his pastoral staff to the King who had given it to him. Whereupon he had proceeded into the Abbey Church, and had stuck his staff into the stone above the Confessor's grave. To the astonishment of everyone it had remained upright and immovable, nor could anyone succeed in drawing it out. Then Wulstan, who had stood aloof, was commanded by the King to approach and resume possession of his staff and See, and forthwith, we are told, the staff yielded to his hand as if it had been merely stuck in clay.

Such stories, and they tended to increase as the years went on, were eagerly collected and cherished by the monks of Westminster, who not unnaturally longed for the canonisation of their founder. In this they could count on the support of the Norman kings whose prestige would be enhanced by the canonisation of the Monarch from whom they claimed to derive their title to the Throne. The much-desired event took place in 1161, and two years later the body of the Saint was translated to a new Shrine within the Abbey. Shortly afterwards Abbot Laurence was granted by the Pope the use of the mitre, ring and gloves, a distinction which placed Westminster among the greater Benedictine Abbeys.

The Cloisters stand on the south side of the Abbey Church, shielded by its walls from the north winds. Here the monks took the air and meditated, and in favourable weather performed some of their daily duties. The more studious read and wrote, while the novices were given their lessons. Above is the South Walk in which are the effigies of three early Abbots. Two—of Gilbert Crispin (d. 1121) and Laurence (d. 1176)—are among the earliest surviving personal effigies in England, and the third commemorates the later Abbot Humez (d. 1222).

The East Walk of the Cloister (*above*) is largely of 13th-century date, the rest being of the 14th century. Through the double arch (*left of the photograph*) is the vestibule of the Chapter House. Beyond are the 'day-stairs' to the monks' Dorter, now the Library, and beyond again is the entrance to the Chapel of the Pyx. The Dark Passage or 'Tunnel' (*below*) and the Undercroft are the only extensive covered remains of the 11th-century monastery. The upper parts of the Cloister windows, (*left*) once glazed, look on to the Cloister Garth or Green.

To Abbot Laurence is also probably due the building or completion of the Chapel of St. Katherine within the Abbey Infirmary, of which the ruins still exist. In this Chapel many councils and episcopal consecrations took place including that of St. Hugh of Lincoln. It was here, too, that the disorderly scene took place in 1176 when the Archbishops of Canterbury and York quarrelled as to who should sit on the right of the Papal Legate, with the deplorable result that both tried to occupy the coveted seat at the same moment. It was an incident in the age-long controversy which was eventually settled by making Canterbury the Primate of All England and York the Primate of England.

The growing prosperity of the Monastery enabled the monks to reconstruct their domestic buildings on a scale worthy of a great Benedictine house. Many of these buildings were again rebuilt during later medieval times, but there still remains the long vaulted Undercroft (c. 1060–1100), which forms the sub-vault to the Dormitory above. At its northern end, but now divided from it, is the Chapel of the Pyx of the same date. This Chapel was once used as the Treasury and derives its name from the chests in which the regalia was kept, and more especially from the Pyx or box which contained the standard gold and silver coins. A door, lined with human skin, of which minute fragments still remain, led from the Chapel to the vestibule of the Chapter House and served as a warning to any who entered the Chapel with unlawful purpose. In the Dormitory above, part of which is now the great Hall of Westminster School, the walls and also some of the windows are of late 11th-century work. So, too, is the lower part of the north wall of the Refectory or Frater, where the monks had their meals, which is also the wall of the South Cloister. In recesses beneath the seat of this Cloister Wall are the graves of three of the early Abbots. The middle one of black Tournai marble represents Abbot Crispin (d. 1117) and is believed to be the earliest example of a recumbent effigy in England.

In general, the lay-out of the Norman monastic buildings followed the usual Benedictine plan, and, in spite of rebuilding, this plan remained constant throughout the monastic period. The monks lived and worked in the North Cloister where they looked due south and had the Abbey Church behind them to shelter them from the north winds. In later days, at any rate, each monk had his own "carrel" or study on the window side where he could work quietly and without interruption. At the west end of this Cloister, as at Durham and elsewhere, are little sets of holes cut in the bench where the Novices could play at marbles. At the other end of the Cloister, against the east wall, stood the great bookcase. In the East Cloister is the Chapter House where the monks transacted business, and beyond are some steps, forming the entrance to the Library, which led to the day-stairs. The two bottom steps can be seen to have been much worn by the feet of those who descended them to the Cloister for the daily round of prayer and work. In the opposite Cloister are the remains of the Lavatorium where the monks washed their hands before proceeding to the Refectory or Frater, which was entered by a door nearby in the South Cloister. Just by the door are the niches where the

Beneath the monks' Dormitory is the long stone-vaulted Undercroft, part of the 11th-century buildings. Partitioned in the Middle Ages, a part is now used as the Abbey Museum (*below*); another section is the Chapel of the Pyx (*above*). This was almost certainly the monastic treasure house in the 14th century. The Pyx, or box, kept in this chamber contained the standard pieces of gold and silver, and here annually took place the trial of the Pyx, the testing of the coinage. It is believed that the State Regalia was kept in the Chapel of the Pyx when in 1649 Parliament ordered that it should be destroyed.

THE WAX EFFIGIES

The most conspicuous exhibits of the Abbey Museum are the wax effigies. Some of these are the actual funeral effigies that were on public view in the Abbey for a short period after the funeral and later stood by the tomb of the deceased, while others, of 18th-century or later origin, were fashioned to provide an attraction for visitors. They are mostly dressed in contemporary clothing, and, indeed, some of the funeral effigies wear the clothing of the persons they depict. Charles II's head (*above*), representative of the funeral effigies, is almost certainly a death mask in painted wax. The effigy of Lord Nelson (*top of page*) wears the vice-admiral's own full-dress coat and was bought so that Westminster might offer a counter-attraction to the naval hero's tomb in St. Paul's Cathedral.

13

towels were kept. The Abbot's Lodgings (now the Deanery) were at the entry to the Cloisters, while the modern Dean's Yard was the Home Farm with the Guest Houses and Cellarer's buildings on one side of it and the Almonry on the other. Finally, well away from the main buildings and between the Cloisters and the Palace, was the Infirmary where the Infirmarer looked after the needs of the sick monks and of the "old stagers" (*Stagiarii*) who were aged and infirm.

It is well to bear all this in mind for it must be remembered that there were monks at Westminster for at least six hundred years, and that far more remains of the monastic buildings than is perhaps generally realised, although many of them are now incorporated in more modern buildings. Practically the whole of the façade of the east side of Dean's Yard, for instance, is original 14th-century work.

The Abbot's Courtyard is surrounded by the buildings of the Abbot's Lodging, the oldest medieval house in London. To the left of the photograph is the 14th-century College Hall. At the foot of the south Western Tower (*seen top right*) are the 14th-century Jerusalem Chamber and 16th-century Jericho Parlour. Between this Courtyard and the Cloister are the rooms now occupied by the Dean of Westminster.

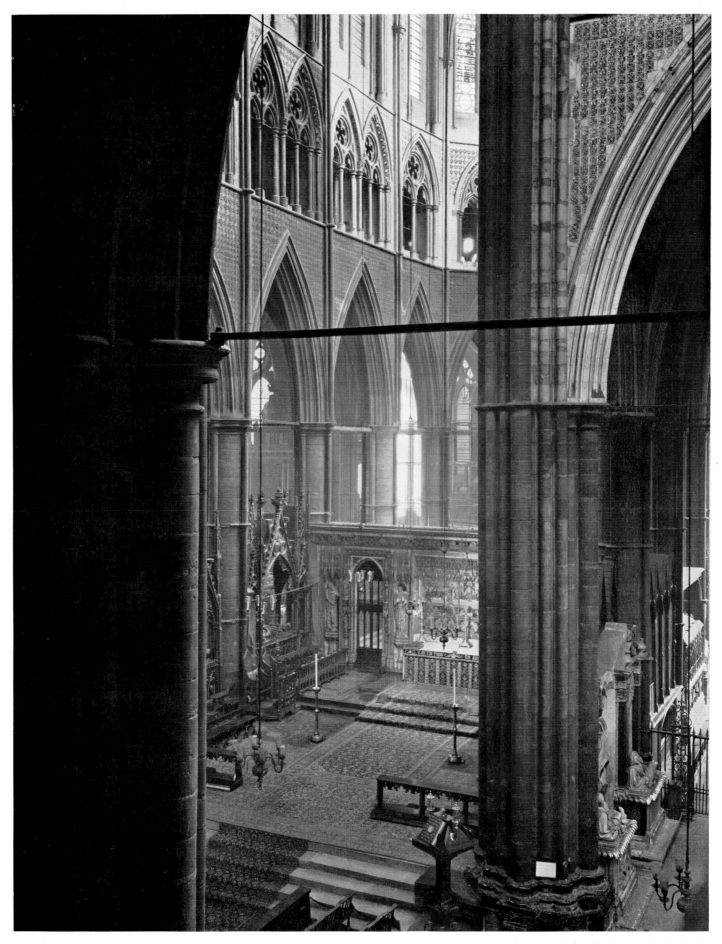

THE SANCTUARY. From this view-point in the Muniment Room in the South Transept a magnificent impression of the Sanctuary and the High Altar is obtained, and the soaring beauty of Henry of Reyns' great arcade may be appreciated to full advantage. The arcade is surmounted by the exquisite triforium and the lofty clerestory. At the bottom right of the photograph are the tombs of Dr. Richard Busby, the famous Head Master of Westminster, and his favourite pupil and friend, Dr. Robert South.

PLAN OF THE ABBEY AND MONASTIC BUILDINGS

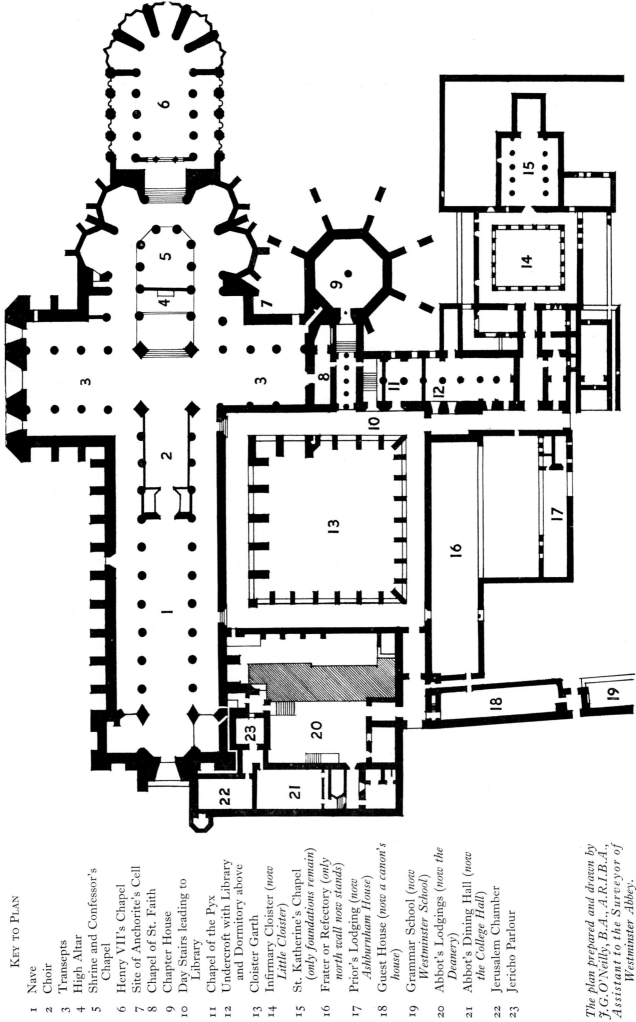

KEY TO PLAN

1 Nave
2 Choir
3 Transepts
4 High Altar
5 Shrine and Confessor's Chapel
6 Henry VII's Chapel
7 Site of Anchorite's Cell
8 Chapel of St. Faith
9 Chapter House
10 Day Stairs leading to Library
11 Chapel of the Pyx
12 Undercroft with Library and Dormitory above
13 Cloister Garth
14 Infirmary Cloister (*now Little Cloister*)
15 St. Katherine's Chapel (*only foundations remain*)
16 Frater or Refectory (*only north wall now stands*)
17 Prior's Lodging (*now Ashburnham House*)
18 Guest House (*now a canon's house*)
19 Grammar School (*now Westminster School*)
20 Abbot's Lodgings (*now the Deanery*)
21 Abbot's Dining Hall (*now the College Hall*)
22 Jerusalem Chamber
23 Jericho Parlour

The plan prepared and drawn by J. G. O'Neilly, B.A., A.R.I.B.A., Assistant to the Surveyor of Westminster Abbey.

16

THE ABBEY OF ST. PETER AND THE PALACE OF WESTMINSTER C. 1532

KEY TO PLAN

1 Westminster Abbey
2 The Palace of Westminster
3 Westminster Hall
4 The Sanctuary
5 The Gatehouse
6 The Mill Stream
7 Long Ditch
8 Chapter House
9 Cloister
10 Dormitory
11 Frater or Refectory
12 Kitchen
13 Prior's Lodging
14 Abbot's Lodging
15 Jerusalem Chamber
16 Guest House
17 Infirmary Cloister
18 St. Katherine's Chapel
19 Infirmary Garden
20 The Home Farm
21 The Granary
22 The Almonry
23 The Belfry
24 The Grammar School
25 King Street
26 Tothill Street
27 Jewel Tower

The reconstruction was drawn by Mr. A. E. Henderson, F.S.A., A.R.I.B.A., after lengthy research in which he was assisted by Mr. Lawrence E. Tanner.

RIVER THAMES

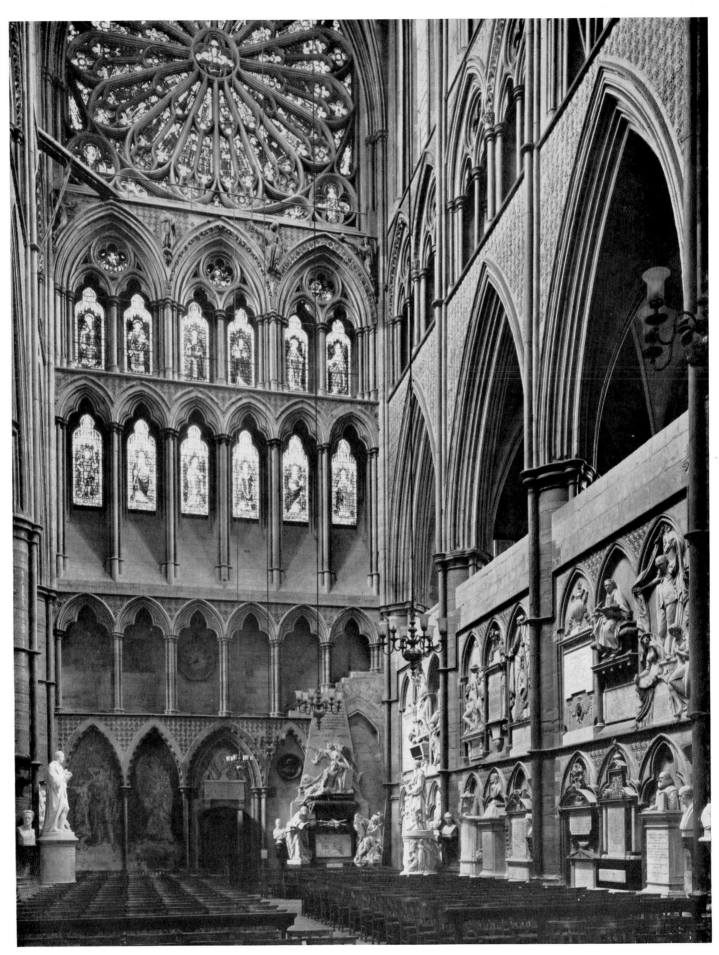

THE SOUTH TRANSEPT. Along the wall of the Muniment Room set in the beautiful 13th-century arcading of the South Transept are many memorials to famous people. On the right are, among others, the monuments of David Garrick, William Camden, Isaac Barrow and Macaulay; beyond, those of Handel and Jenny Lind, the singer. Against the end wall is the tomb of the Duke of Argyll by Roubiliac. This monument partially covers the doorway of the monks' 'night stairs,' from their dormitory.

2

HENRY III's ABBEY CHURCH

E have seen that the Confessor's Church, whether wholly completed or not, was consecrated in 1065. It was to stand for nearly two hundred years. In 1220, in order to satisfy the devotional needs of the time, a Lady Chapel was added at its eastern end. The foundation stone was laid on 16th May of that year by the young King, Henry III. It was the eve of his Coronation, and he gave towards the cost of the work the gold spurs which were used during the ceremony on the following day. But the Chapel was not a specially Royal foundation, and a large number of documents preserved among the Abbey Muniments show that it was built largely from the gifts of the faithful to whom spiritual benefits were promised in return for their part in forwarding the work. The Chapel seems to have been completed about 1240–45. No trace of it now remains for it was to be swept away when Henry VII built his Chapel on the site at the beginning of the 16th century.

How far this Lady Chapel may be considered as an addition to the Confessor's Church or, on the other hand, as the first step towards the general rebuilding of the whole Church must remain in doubt. It is interesting to remember that the foundation stone of the new cathedral at Salisbury was laid in the same year, and there has always been a tradition that it was the beauty and grace of Salisbury which first suggested to Henry the idea of replacing the massive solidity of the Confessor's Church with a building more in the spirit of the age. The soaring tendency symbolised by the pointed arch, which was to find its fullest expression in the great French cathedrals of l'Ile de France, was evidently fascinating Henry and his contemporaries, although it had to contend with other influences and with a sturdy conservatism which was prepared to assimilate but not blindly to copy French ideas. The result at Westminster was a Church which was a mixture of French and English influences. The Master Mason or architect, Henry of Reyns, who designed the Church, was almost certainly an Englishman; so, too, were his successors John of Gloucester and Robert of Beverley, and all of them employed English craftsmen. Henry of Reyns, unquestionably, had profoundly studied the great cathedrals of Amiens and Reims, and in his design for Westminster he was prepared to adopt and adapt such features of those cathedrals as seemed good to him.

He took, for instance, his plan, with its radiating eastern chapels, from Reims; and his proportions—the lovely pointed arches, Triforium and Clerestory —from Amiens. He was obviously fascinated also by the great circular windows, so distinctively French, and he copied them in the "Rose" Windows in the Transepts at Westminster. So, too, with the flying buttresses which take the weight of the Church. But if these are French features, the great length of the Transepts, the actual form of the Triforium and the polygonal Chapter House are no less distinctively English. In the end he produced a building which has never ceased to fascinate those who have studied it, "a great French thought," as Sir Gilbert Scott called it, "expressed in excellent English."

In one respect Westminster is a landmark in the architectural history of the Middle Ages in England. The extent and variety of its interior decoration was unique and was profoundly to influence the future. As it has been pointed out Westminster is "the most sumptuously decorated Gothic building in Europe with one exception, the Sainte Chapelle at Paris, and it is probable that King Henry's intention was to reproduce the jewel-box-like character of St. Louis's chapel on the scale of a full-size church."[1] This is the more likely for it is clear that apart from interior decoration there are, as the late Professor Lethaby showed, striking correspondences in architectural details between Westminster and the Sainte Chapelle.

In planning the Church Henry of Reyns had to bear in mind that Westminster was both a monastic and a Royal church. He had always to remember that the needs of the monks came first. He had to ensure that they could get easily from the monastic buildings to the Choir, that they had sufficient side chapels and altars and that the crowds of pilgrims who came to visit the Shrine could be dealt with easily and without disturbing the privacy of the daily routine. Here, of course, the fact that he was dealing with a monastery already in existence both simplified and complicated his work. The general plan was already laid down, but he had to fit his church to the existing monastic buildings, and this limited the space at his disposal.

In order, for instance, to get space for his lengthened Transepts with their aisles (a new feature), he contrived that the Chapter House should be pushed further to the east and south and entered by a vaulted vestibule under the Dormitory. He was thus able to extend his South Transept, and, by a brilliant inspiration, made a kind of upper aisle to the Transept by roofing over the Cloister and forming a gallery above it (now the Muniment Room) looking down into the Church. Access to the Choir, which was shut off from the rest of the Church by the monks' stalls and by some form of screen across the Transepts, was through the east and west Cloister Doors, and to enable the monks to get easily from their Dormitory to the Church for the night offices a bridge was built across

[1] Geoffrey Webb. *Gothic Architecture in England*, p. 18.

The incomparable effects of interplaying light and shade among the windows and arcades of the Sanctuary and the North Transept can be clearly seen in this exceptional study taken from the Muniment Room. The more immoderate monuments of the 18th and 19th centuries in no way dominate the scene beneath the soaring columns and high vaults.

the west end of St. Faith's Chapel from which they could descend by the night stairs into the South Transept. The stairs have gone but the arch of the door which led to them can be seen behind the monument to the Duke of Argyll, at the south end of the Transept.

The radiating Chapels and the east aisle of the North Transept provided space for the numerous altars required in a great Benedictine Monastery. But the west aisle of the North Transept was left empty, for it was through the door to this aisle that pilgrims entered the Church. Thence they could be shepherded round the ambulatories seeing, as they passed, the Shrine and the backs of the Royal tombs, and returning the way they came. Probably only the more distinguished were admitted into the Confessor's Chapel.

But Westminster was not only a monastic church, it was also the Coronation Church. For this purpose the architect deliberately placed his Choir west of the central crossing. This had, indeed, been a feature of the Confessor's Church and it was also a feature of the French Coronation Church of Reims. By doing this the platform of the "theatre," as it is called, on which the Coronation takes place could be erected in the central crossing, and this, with the Transepts, provided adequate space for those who attended a medieval Coronation. For all great functions in medieval times the State entrance to the Abbey was through the North Door and not, as is more usual in English churches, through the West Door. It was nearer the Palace, and it looked towards the main approach from London. For this reason the north façade with its three porches, which derive from similar porches at Amiens, is much more imposing and elaborate than the façade above the great West Door. On less important occasions the Sovereign would come across from the Palace and enter by the small door in what is now Poets' Corner, and take his place in the Royal Pew (the "King's Cage" as it was called) which occupied the site of the tomb of Anne of Cleves on the south side of the Sanctuary by the High Altar.

The eastern part of the Confessor's Church was pulled down in July 1245, and from that date until his death, about 1254, Henry of Reyns was in charge of the rebuilding. In this period probably the whole of the eastern part of the existing Church was built together with the Transepts and the Chapter House. Henry of Reyns was succeeded as Master Mason by John of Gloucester who held the office until about 1260–61. There are indications that under him the work slackened slightly. He was engaged on much other work at the time and would appear to have been often away. In 1258, however, the building of the Choir west of the central crossing seems to have begun, and this was carried to its conclusion by his successor, Robert of Beverley. He appears to have lived almost continuously at Westminster from 1260 to 1269 and to have devoted most of his attention to the work in hand. The late Professor Lethaby thought that on the evidence of the fabric itself "all that is distinctive in the character of the second work must be ascribed to Master Robert." There is evidence that the King was full of anxiety to press on with the building, and it is probable that the first five

ST. EDWARD'S SHRINE

The Abbey Church of King Edward the Confessor was consecrated on 28th December, 1065, as the King lay grievously ill in the Palace of Westminster. Eight days later he died, and the poignant scene at his deathbed was later embroidered into the Bayeux Tapestry, a section from which is reproduced below. Around the King are Edith, his Queen, and Harold, his successor, and perhaps the Archbishop. The Confessor was first buried before the High Altar of his new church, but in 1163 his remains were translated to a shrine raised by Henry II. Here they lay until 1245 when Henry III commenced to pull down the Norman church. This first shrine was removed and a more magnificent one prepared which was to become the wonder of England. Expert workers in glass mosaic and marble tesseræ were imported from Rome, and Henry III beggared himself in his endeavours to adorn the Shrine with jewels and precious metals. Twice despoilers have stripped the tomb of its riches, and today only a slight impression may be gained of its former glory. Nevertheless the Confessor's Shrine (*right*) is still the most sacred spot in the Abbey. In the arched recesses of the Shrine sick people were once left overnight to be cured by the Saint, and at one end the stone steps (*below*) are worn into hollows by the knees of countless pilgrims. Catholics still make pilgrimages to the Shrine.

23

bays west of the crossing (i.e. one bay beyond the Choir Screen) were practically complete by 13th October, 1269, when the Church was consecrated and the body of the Confessor was translated to a new Shrine behind the High Altar.

This was the limit of the building under Henry III. The Nave of the Confessor's Church was left untouched, linked in some way to the new Church, until it was pulled down some hundred years later.

The Censing Angels in the South Transept are the supreme examples of 13th-century art within the Abbey Church, masterly in conception and perfect in poise and grace. They are, perhaps, the loveliest things of their kind in England and are equal to anything found in French cathedrals. The Angels were once brightly coloured.

The beautiful head above with the attitude and expression of quiet contemplation is a remarkable example of Greek feeling, and perhaps influence, in 13th-century English sculpture. It is commonly known as "The Thinker" and has been described as a likeness of Master Henry de Reyns but with no real justification. The carved head of a youth wearing a prince's coronet (*below*) was formerly believed to be a portrait of Henry III, who, however, at the time the head was fashioned was a middle-aged man. This, the only marble portrait in the Abbey, is inside the central Royal porch of the North Transept. It is now thought to be a contemporary portrait of the young Prince Edward, afterwards, Edward I.

THE CHAPEL OF ST. FAITH

The Chapel of St. Faith stands between the South Transept and the vestibule of the Chapter House. Formerly a vestry for the monks, it is now a chapel for meditation and prayer, and is occasionally used for confirmations, marriages and funerals. There are still preserved on the floor at the east end the original 13th-century glazed tiles, and over the altar, dedicated to St. Faith, is a remarkable wall painting, also of the 13th century. It represents St. Faith, wearing a crown and holding a book and a gridiron, the emblem of her martyrdom. Below this painting is a Crucifixion, while on the left-hand wall is a small half-figure of a praying monk, possibly a self-portrait of the artist. On the western wall traces remain of a rack on which copes and other vestments were hung. Across the west end of the Chapel is a gallery between the Dormitory and the ' night-stairs ' into the South Transept. When the stonework of the Chapel was cleaned in 1937, the series of corbels that support the groined vault were revealed to be finely carved studies of human heads. The irregular shape of St. Faith's Chapel is due to its situation between the great buttresses and walls of the South Transept.

THE NORTH TRANSEPT. Through this transept was the principal
public entrance, especially for pilgrims, to the Abbey Church.
Its external face has been frequently and radically restored,
notably by Wren and J. L. Pearson. The interior has been
scarcely affected though the Rose Window, which contains much
of Sir James Thornhill's painted glass of 1722, was restored
by Pearson from the designs of Sir Gilbert Scott. The North
Transept is sometimes called the Statesmen's Aisle.

THE SOUTH TRANSEPT. The transepts are early parts of Henry III's new church. They are remarkable for their great Rose Windows high above tiers of graceful arches, and although that in the South Transept has been restored several times the pattern of its stonework remains substantially unchanged. In the spandrels just below this Rose Window, in the corners, are the two Censing Angels; between are mutilated figures, presumably those of St. Edward the Confessor and the Pilgrim.

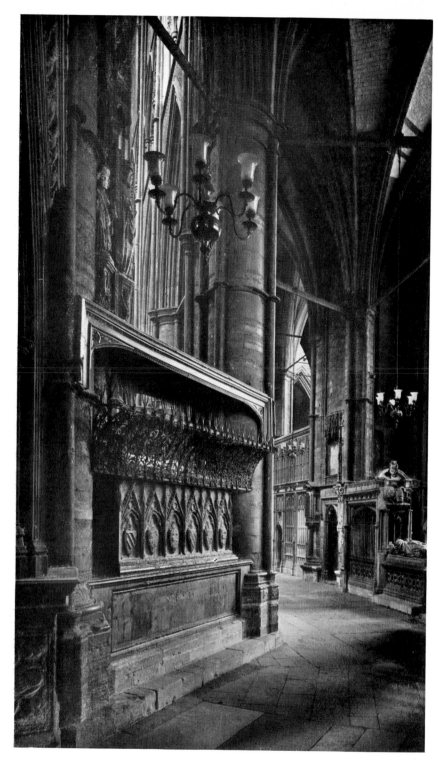

The tomb of Henry III (*above*) stands in the Confessor's Chapel. Of Purbeck marble, it is raised on a pedestal once entirely decorated with mosaic work by Peter the Roman. The tomb has set in each side a slab of red porphyry surrounded by a mosaic border, and at the corners are twisted shafts. On the tomb lies the recumbent gilt bronze effigy of the King, dressed in Coronation robes with a crown which originally contained jewels. The effigy (*below*) was made by William Torel in 1291.

THE NORTH AMBULATORY

Henry III's Abbey Church was partly designed to provide for pilgrimages to the Confessor's Shrine and the many Holy Relics. After entering through the North Transept, the medieval pilgrims would pass through the North Ambulatory (*above*) and walk the whole way round the Chapel of St. Edward. On proper Feast Days they would be allowed access to the Shrine itself where the sick would seek relief through the Saint's thaumaturgical gifts and the pilgrims make their devotions. Strong wooden or stone screens protected the chapels and their monuments from casual desecration. This part of the monastic church was probably the most frequented by the lay public. On the left of the photograph is the tomb of Eleanor of Castile with its beautiful wrought-iron grille (*see page 31*). Below it are shields with the coats of arms of England, Castile and Leon, and Ponthieu. On the base is a carved panel on which faint traces remain of a painting of a knight kneeling before a woman bearing a child in her arms, presumably Our Lady, and four pilgrims praying at a tomb.

3

THE JEWEL AND ITS SETTING

THE cult of St. Edward reached its height during the reign of King Henry III. This was due very largely to the King himself who seems to have deliberately taken the Confessor as a model, and not only called his eldest son after him but surrounded himself with representations of the Saint in stone, glass and painting in all his Palaces. It was inevitable, therefore, that the new Church at Westminster should have had as its chief object, after the worship of God, the glorification of St. Edward. The Shrine which the King had had made to contain the body of the Saint was the jewel to which all else was the setting.

The Abbot of Westminster, Richard de Ware, was in Rome in 1259 and again in 1267, and it was from Rome that he brought back the craftsmen who made the Shrine and the pavement in front of the High Altar. The pavement is of red and green porphyry and glass mosaic, inlaid in Purbeck marble. On it were three inscriptions of which a few isolated single letters still remain. The first of these was round the circular stone in the centre of the pavement, and it stated that this stone represented the Universe because the porphyry of which it was composed contained the four colours of the elements—fire, air, water, earth. The second inscription was a curious prophetic calculation of the duration of the world, which by taking the supposed average age of man, bird, beast and fish and by adding them together was made to come to an end in the year 19,683. The third and last inscription stated that in 1268 King Henry III, the City (i.e. Rome), Odoricus (the mosaic worker) and the Abbot "assembled these porphyry stones together." This wonderful example of the art of the Roman Cosmati School is unique in England, although there are pavements in Rome and elsewhere in Italy which closely resemble it. It is not improbable that it was a present from the Pope, Clement IV, to Henry's new Church.

Rising behind it, although now separated from it by the 15th-century Altar Screen, is the great Shrine of St. Edward, which seems to have been completed by 1269. This also was the work of the Cosmati and was made, as the inscription on it formerly stated, by Peter, the Roman citizen. The Shrine consists of a rectangular Purbeck-marble base with recesses in the sides surmounted formerly by a golden feretory beneath which rested the body of the Saint. The feretory is now replaced by a 16th-century wooden superstructure. The whole of the Purbeck-marble base, with the twisted columns at the angles, was originally covered with mosaic decoration of which very little now remains. The coffin containing the body of the Saint is above the recesses so that those who came to pray at the Shrine could kneel beneath it. At the east end the step is worn into two deep hollows showing where people knelt. Near the west end of the cornice on each side are removable stones which enabled objects to be passed from one side to the other and to touch the head of the coffin as they passed. Many little scratched crosses within the recesses were probably made by pilgrims to mark the end of their pilgrimage. At the west end are two twisted columns which now support the reredos slab of the Altar. But originally these columns stood separately on each side of the Altar and carried figures of the Confessor and St. John. As they are now placed part of each pillar is buried underground, but Sir Gilbert Scott opened the ground and turned one of the pillars upside down thereby revealing much of the original mosaic work. This wonderful Shrine, which is and always must be the central thing in the Abbey, is the only important Shrine in England which still remains and still contains the body of its Saint. No doubt the fact that the Saint had also been a King saved it from complete destruction at the Reformation, although it was evidently altered and partially reset at that time.

The Shrine was, as has been said, the jewel to which all else was the setting, but the setting was such as no other church in England could rival. On the internal decoration of the Church Henry III and the craftsmen he employed lavished all their wealth and skill. Among the Muniments at the Abbey is an extraordinarily interesting collection of contemporary documents dealing with the houses and lands of these craftsmen. These documents show that they settled in the neighbourhood in order to be near the great work they had in hand. It is fascinating to turn these documents over, and to know that they were originally handled by the very men who, as we know from the account rolls, were building and adorning the Abbey Church—such great craftsmen as Odo the Goldsmith and his son Edward, Alexander the Carpenter, John of St. Alban's the Sculptor, Henry the Glazier and the rest. And even more interesting are those documents which were attested by, or dealt with, the properties of the three Master Masons, Henry of Reyns, John of Gloucester and Robert of Beverley. Thus among them, to give but one example, is a deed dated 20th March, 1261, by which Hugh, son of the late Master Henry de Reyns, Master Mason (*Cementarius*) granted to Richard the Abbot, and to the monks of Westminster "a rent of five shillings from a messuage in Westminster held by Walter le Imager (Sculptor) and given to the said Hugh by his Father Henry . . . in order to support a lamp before St. Mary's Altar in the Church of Westminster."

It was John of St. Alban's and his craftsmen who carved the two figures of angels swinging censers high up in the spandrels under the great Rose Window in the South Transept. These entrancing figures, so lovely in their serenity and

30

ROYAL EFFIGIES

Eleanor of Castile, the first wife of Edward I, died in Nottinghamshire in 1290, and the halting places on the route of her funeral progress to London are marked by the famous Eleanor Crosses, one of which gave its name to Charing Cross. On her Purbeck-marble tomb in the Chapel of the Kings was placed the gilt bronze effigy by William Torel, seen above. Formerly Queen Eleanor held a sceptre in her right hand. On the north side of her tomb is a superbly fashioned wrought-iron grille made by Thomas of Leighton, and above is a 15th-century wooden tester. In St. Edmund's Chapel stands the tomb of William de Valence, a half-brother of Henry III, who died in 1296. This tomb is notable as the only example in England decorated with Limoges enamel work. Formerly the whole of the copper-covered oak effigy (*left*) and the oak part of the tomb were adorned with glittering enamel of which only a few fragments remain. Below is reproduced a section of the wrought-iron grille of Queen Eleanor's tomb.

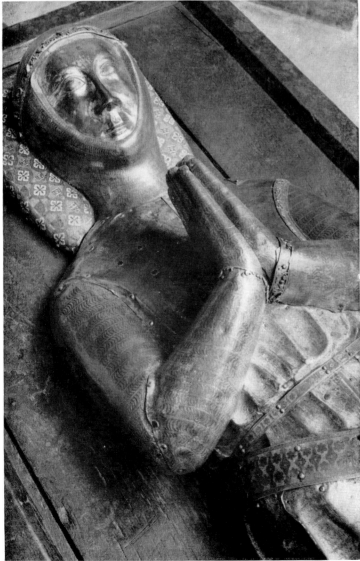

poise, need fear no comparison with anything in France or Europe of that date. They are supreme examples of 13th-century art. They had, indeed, long been recognised as such, but it was a complete surprise to find some few years ago, when it was possible to examine them closely, that in spite of their great height from the ground—some 80 feet or more—not only had their robes and wings been brightly coloured but also even their cheeks and the pupils of their eyes.

These same sculptors probably were responsible also for the slightly more austere but strikingly beautiful figures on each side of the Chapter House Doorway representing the Annunciation. All these are major works of art, but in many of the corbel heads, notably in St. Faith's Chapel, and in the curving foliage of the capitals there is a beauty which is entrancing, and this has become more apparent in recent years as they have been freed from the grime and dirt with which they had become encrusted. Notable, too, are the fine series of stone shields, carved and painted with the coats of arms of the leading men of the time, which are in the spandrels of the wall arcade in the Choir Aisles.

Of the 13th-century glass which must once have been one of the glories of the Church all that remains are seven small panels of scenes from the Gospels, now in the window of the Jerusalem Chamber, some fragments of grisaille and some patched-up heraldic shields. On the other hand Westminster is rich in 13th-century mural and other paintings. These paintings date from the last half of the century, and, although their exact date is a matter of controversy, it is reasonable to suppose that they would have been executed shortly after the consecration of the Church in 1269. The most striking, and probably the earliest, is the large painting of St. Faith over the Altar in the Chapel which is dedicated to her. There is an impressive austerity and beauty about this tall crowned figure which is in striking contrast to the barbaric gold-and-jewel-encrusted figure of the same Saint, dating from the 10th century, which is still preserved at Conques in the south of France.

More curious, inasmuch as their existence was entirely unsuspected until a few years ago, are the paintings representing St. Christopher and the Incredulity of St. Thomas on the south wall of the South Transept. These great paintings had been hidden partly by two 18th-century monuments, partly by dirt and by a preservative which had been put at some time over the dirt. The figures are nearly 9 feet high and were probably two of a series of which the others are irretrievably lost. They are the work of a great master, and they have been ascribed to Walter of Durham, the King's painter.

It has been suggested that there are close affinities between these paintings and those on the Retable, as it is usually called, which is now preserved in the south Ambulatory. The Retable is of oak. It has elaborate gesso and coloured-glass decoration and is often supposed to have been made for the original High Altar. There are, however, objections to this theory inasmuch as it seems improbable that an object so important would not have been decorated with precious metals and real jewels. The late Professor Tristram thought that it might have

In the 15th century a great carved stone screen was erected between the Sanctuary and the Chapel of St. Edward. Against the west side stands the High Altar (*above*) at which all the important Abbey services are celebrated. This side was heavily restored in 1867 after Sir Gilbert Scott's design. The mosaic above the High Altar represents the Last Supper. The east side (*below*) though seriously defaced, still offers some impression of the wonderfully delicate carving. Here, in St. Edward's Chapel, stands the historic Coronation Chair constructed to the order of Edward I in 1300 to contain the Stone of Scone. It was once richly decorated. To the left of the Coronation Chair may be seen the sword and shield said to have belonged to Edward III.

33

been one of the sides of the wooden canopy which normally hung over the Shrine, and he pointed out that measurements showed that it would have been exactly fitted for this purpose. However this may be it is a supreme work of art of the 13th century, and the delicacy and technical excellence of the paintings with which it is adorned are unrivalled for the period. It is sadly mutilated, and for centuries it was used as the top of one of the cupboards in which were kept the wax effigies. It was found in this position and rescued just over a century ago.

Whether King Henry III lived to see all the beautiful things with which his Church was being adorned must remain in doubt. He died in 1272 and his splendid tomb on the north side of the Shrine is the work of the Cosmati craftsmen who had worked on the Shrine and the pavement in the Sanctuary. It is purely Italian in conception, and the mosaic work on it is strikingly like that on the tombs of Popes Clement IV (d. 1268) and Adrian V (d. 1276) at Viterbo. The view of the tomb looking across the Ambulatory from St. John the Baptist's Chapel gives some idea of its original splendour with its brilliant mosaics and slabs of red porphyry. These great slabs of imperial porphyry cannot be later in date than the 6th century, when the quarry in Egypt ceased to be worked, and they must have been brought by the Italian craftsmen from the ruins of Rome where they found the materials they used in their work. Rather than cut them the slabs have been forced into the foliated iron clips which hold them and have been cracked in the process. In the pillar just behind the head of the effigy there is cut a little niche about six inches high, and there can be little doubt that it once contained the phial of the Holy Blood which was sent to Henry III by the Patriarch of Jerusalem and which the King carried barefoot through the streets of London to the Abbey. The actual tomb seems to have been completed by 1290, and the noble gilt bronze effigy by William Torel was in place by 1292.

At the same time Torel was at work on the lovely effigy of Henry's daughter-in-law, Queen Eleanor of Castile, the first wife of King Edward I. The Purbeck-marble tomb, on which the bronze effigy is placed, is purely English and was the work of Richard de Crundale who had been working on the "Eleanor" Crosses which marked the resting places of the Queen's body on its way from Nottinghamshire to Westminster. Particularly charming are the little lions on which the Queen's feet rest, and the noble wrought-iron grille, the work of Thomas de Leighton, which protects the tomb on the Ambulatory side. English, too, and probably from a London workshop, is the beautiful effigy of Aveline, Countess of Lancaster (d. 1273), on the north side of the Sanctuary by the High Altar. The tomb is far less elaborate than the slightly later one to her husband, Crouchback, nearby. It dates from the last decade of the 13th century, and the graceful flowing lines of the drapery are reminiscent of the figures on the Eleanor Crosses. It bears a marked resemblance to a slightly earlier effigy to Lady FitzAlan (c. 1280) in Chichester Cathedral.

In striking contrast is the enamelled effigy of William de Valence (d. 1296),

34

THE SANCTUARY TOMBS

The three tombs in the Sanctuary seen above are rare examples of medieval craftsmanship. Each has a recumbent effigy surrounded by carved "weepers" or mourners in niches, and above are ornate canopies. The tomb on the left of the photograph, of Aveline, Countess of Lancaster, who died about 1273, is the earliest. Her husband, Edmund Crouchback, the Earl of Lancaster, second son of Henry III, who died in 1296, lies in the tomb adjacent to the altar screen. Between is the tomb of Aymer de Valence, Earl of Pembroke, a cousin of Edward I. The two earls are represented in full armour, and Aveline is attired in the costume of her time, a long mantle and wimple. All three tombs were once richly coloured and decorated but are now much faded. The 17th-century pulpit is seen left of the photograph. On the opposite side of the Sanctuary stand the Sedilia (*right*) erected over Sebert's tomb. It dates from the reign of Edward I; only two of the original four figures painted on the backboard remain. These probably depict Henry III and Edward I. The central carved head on the canopy is possibly that of Abbot Walter de Wenlock (1283-1307).

the half-brother of Henry III, in St. Edmund's Chapel.   It is of oak, covered with thin copper plates partly engraved and partly covered with diaper in Limoges champlevé enamel.   The effigy is in armour, the surcoat powdered with little shields of the Valence and other coats of arms.   The tomb has been much mutilated but the superb full-sized shield with the Valence martlets on the left side is perfect and undamaged.   The whole tomb was probably imported from Limoges and is similar in workmanship to the tomb of Blanche of Castile (d. 1283) now in the Louvre.

At the close of the century two notable additions were made to the furnishing of the Abbey Church.   In 1300–01 the Coronation Chair was made at a cost of one hundred shillings to enclose the Scottish Stone of Scone.   The Chair is of oak and was formerly enriched with gilt gesso decoration and glass mosaics. Master Walter of Durham was engaged on the work, and there are remains of the design of a throned king on the inner face behind the seat as well as panels containing birds and foliage on the sides of the Chair, although it is possible that some of this decoration may be of slightly later date.   The Chair has been used at every Coronation since that of Edward II.   It has been shamefully treated in the past and names have been cut all over it.   Beneath is the Stone of Scone upon which Jacob is said to have laid his head and dreamed his dream.   It would appear, in fact, to have been originally quarried in Perthshire or Angus and its known history begins in 1249 when it is stated to have been used at the Coronation of King Alexander III of Scotland.   It was captured by Edward I in 1296 and brought to Westminster where, since that time, Chair and Stone have come down the centuries together with their historic associations inextricably intertwined.

A few years later (*c.* 1300) the oak Sedilia were added on the south side of the High Altar, probably by Abbot Walter de Wenlock.   On the side of the Sedilia towards the Altar are two large paintings of kings which appear to represent founders of the Church.   They are probably the work of Master Thomas, the son of Walter of Durham.   A charming little carved and painted mitred head on the pendant of one of the stalls is doubtless a portrait of Abbot Walter.   Recent cleaning has revealed on the back of the Sedilia towards the Ambulatory a figure of Edward the Confessor and the mutilated remains of an Annunciation.

Two of the weepers on the base of the tomb of Edmund Crouchback, Earl of Lancaster (*see page* 35). This detailed picture shows delicate and skilful 13th-century carving, once highly coloured.

THE CHAPEL OF ST. EDMUND

St. Edmund's Chapel is separated from the South Ambulatory by a 15th-century wooden screen. To the left of the photograph above, a corner of the tomb of William de Valence (*see page* 31) may be seen; to the right of the gate is that of John of Eltham, Earl of Cornwall, second son of Edward II who died at Perth in 1337, aged nineteen. His effigy and tomb are of alabaster, once coloured. The effigy is of particular historical interest as it offers details of the mixed mail and plate armour of the period. The feet rest on a lion; two angels support the head cushion. John of Eltham's shield bears the arms of England with a border of French heraldic symbols. Formerly the tomb was surmounted by a triple canopy which, unfortunately, was destroyed in 1776. In the niches on the sides of the base are figures of the English and French kings and queens to whom he was related. By the side is a small tomb of two infant children of Edward III, William de Windsor and Blanche de la Tour (d. 1340). The alabaster effigies, only twenty inches long, are dressed as children of older years. In the foreground of the photograph is a fine brass to Eleanor, Duchess of Gloucester (d. 1399) the greatest heiress of her time in England, and against the pillar is the monument to Mary, Countess of Stafford in her own right (d. 1694).

The pair of lions seen centre, left, support the feet of the 13th-century gilt bronze effigy of Queen Eleanor of Castile (*see page* 31). Below is one of the heraldic shields in the soffits of the arcading of the 13th-century bays of the Nave. The shield with the double-tailed lion is that of Simon de Montfort, who married Eleanor, a sister of Henry III.

SIMON LANGHAM

In St. Benedict's Chapel in the South Ambulatory stand the tombs of Cardinal Simon Langham (*left*) and Dean Gabriel Goodman (*below, right*). The effigy and tomb of the Cardinal are of alabaster, and he is represented wearing mass vestments, formerly bejewelled, his feet resting on a small dog with a collar of bells. Cardinal Langham's remarkable career as Abbot of Westminster, Bishop of Ely, Lord Chancellor, Archbishop of Canterbury, Cardinal and Cardinal Bishop of Palestrina is recorded in the coats of arms on the tomb. He was the prime mover in the rebuilding of the Nave, and after he died at Avignon in 1374 his great fortune passed to the Abbey. Dr. Gabriel Goodman (d. 1601) was Dean of Westminster for forty years in the reign of Queen Elizabeth I. Founder of Christ's Hospital and the Ruthin Grammar School, he was also a benefactor of several Cambridge Colleges. His monument shows him kneeling at a prayer-desk in full robes and skull-cap. The prayer-desk conceals a hole which was a window of the Anchorite's cell; the doorway at the side of the tomb probably led to the cell.

On each side of the magnificent gabled canopy over the tomb of Edmund Crouchback, Earl of Lancaster in the sanctuary, is a trefoiled panel containing a figure of the Earl praying on horseback (*below, left*). The Earl is depicted in the chain-mail armour of his time.

THE PORTRAIT OF RICHARD II

This contemporary portrait of Richard II, though overpainted, was largely restored to its original state in the mid-19th century by George Richmond, R.A. It is believed to have been presented to the Abbey by the King himself, and is generally held to be the work of André Beauneveu of Valenciennes who painted at the English Court until about 1398. The picture shows Richard seated in King Edward's Chair. He is attired in his Parliamentary robes of crimson lined with ermine over a green vest powdered with the gold letter " R," an ermine cape, vermilion socks and gilt shoes. He wears St. Edward's Crown and is holding the Orb surmounted by the Cross in his right hand and a rod with fleurs-de-lys in his left. The portrait represents the King as quite a young man. The background was once a pattern of raised and gilt gesso work of which only a few fragments remain; the frame is modern. This, the earliest-known painted likeness of an English king, now hangs near St. George's Chapel in the Nave, but for long it hung in the Choir where it was greatly injured by the wigs of those who sat by it. In 1775 the painting was put in the Jerusalem Chamber and later transferred to the Sanctuary by Dean Stanley, where it remained for many years. It is interesting to compare the portrait with the head of the gilt bronze effigy of the King (below); the resemblance is striking.

The head of Richard II from the gilt bronze effigy on his tomb in the Chapel of the Kings (*right*) is undoubtedly an authentic likeness of the King. By his wish Richard II was represented holding the right hand of his beloved first wife, Anne, tenderly in his, but both arms have long since been stolen. The effigy was executed in 1397 after the Queen's death and in the King's lifetime by the London coppersmiths Nicholas Broker and Godfrey Prest.

THE GREAT WEST WINDOW. The western part of the Abbey was rebuilt late in the 14th century, and was finished not long before the Dissolution of the Monastery in 1540. Here is continued the design of the earlier work at the east end. The great West Window, inserted late in the 15th century, contains glass painted by Joshua Price in 1735, designed, perhaps, by Sir James Thornhill. Below the window, over the West Door, is a monument to William Pitt, the Younger, the illustrious Prime Minister.

4

THE MEDIEVAL TOMBS: THE NEW NAVE

THE 13th century had seen the building of the Church and its internal adornment. The century which followed was notable for the Royal and other tombs which were erected within its walls. They form, indeed, a series, spanning the century, unrivalled by any other church in the country. But this was not all. Towards the end of the century began the great work of entirely rebuilding the Nave of the Abbey Church as well as many of the conventual buildings within the precincts.

It will be convenient first to deal with the tombs. The perfectly plain Purbeck-marble tomb of Edward I (d. 1307) is in striking contrast not only to the nearby tomb of his wife, Eleanor of Castile, but also to that of his brother, Edmund Crouchback, Earl of Lancaster. The contrast with the latter must, indeed, have been even more striking before the erection of the 15th-century Altar Screen which now divides the two tombs. No one knows the reason for this rectangular altar-tomb without ornament or effigy. It may have been so erected in accordance with the King's own wishes, or, on the other hand, Edward II may have failed, in this, as in so much else, to show respect to his father's memory. It did, indeed, originally have a canopy or tester over it, but this was torn down in a riot which occurred at an 18th-century funeral.

The tomb of his brother Crouchback, with its triple-arched canopy and "weepers" has been described as "the most splendid medieval tomb in England." The effigy, in surcoat and mail, and the whole tomb have been elaborately painted and much of this remains and has been brought out by cleaning. In the gable of the canopy is a charming little representation of Crouchback on horseback, pink cheeked and blue eyed, praying, "his hands and head given to God, and his knees still keeping a firm grip on his mount." [1] The tomb must date from about the turn of the century and was probably the work of Crundale and Alexander of Abingdon, who had recently completed their work on the Eleanor Crosses.

Slightly later, but still in the shrine-like tradition, is the adjoining tomb of Aymer de Valence, Earl of Pembroke (d. 1324), Crouchback's cousin. The tomb is really a copy of Crouchback's, although less elaborate. At the head of

---

[1] Joan Evans. *English Art 1307–1461*, p. 6.

his effigy two mutilated angels support his soul. Fifty years after his death, his widow, the Foundress of Pembroke College, Cambridge, left money in her will for masses to be said for his soul and hers every day *"en la chapelle près de la sepulture de mon tres cher seigneur Monsieur Aymar de Valence."* This must be the Chapel of Our Lady of the Pew which had then recently been constructed in the thickness of the wall between the Chapel of St. John the Baptist and that of Abbot Islip. It now forms the entry to the Chapel of St. John, but originally it was a separate Chapel. It has its original 14th-century gates, and the niche for the statue of Our Lady together with much of the original painting on the walls still remain.

Hitherto effigies on tombs had been mainly of Purbeck marble or stone, made more lifelike by the elaborate use of paint and gesso. The highest point was perhaps reached in the Crouchback and Valence tombs at Westminster and the tomb of Bishop Bronescombe (d. 1280) at Exeter. But in the first half of the 14th century it was discovered that paint could be equally well used on alabaster which was softer and less difficult to carve, although it could hardly be foreseen that ultimately the paint would tend to disappear and that the effigy itself would become the prey of the penknife of the vandal. Westminster was quick to reflect the newest fashion. The fine alabaster tomb to Prince John of Eltham (d. 1337) in St. Edmund's Chapel owed its inspiration to the tomb of his father, Edward II, in Gloucester Cathedral, and was probably from the same workshop. The effigy of the Prince is a very noble one. Clad in mail, his head supported by two angels, he bears upon his left arm a superbly carved shield with the Royal arms. Round the base of the tomb are very delightful, if slightly mannered, "weepers." The tomb, like that of his father, was formerly surmounted by a canopy. Drawings of this canopy exist, but the canopy itself collapsed when spectators clambered upon it at the funeral of the Duchess of Northumberland in 1776.

John of Eltham's tomb was English work, but the tomb of his sister-in-law, Queen Philippa (d. 1369), was foreign in conception. The effigy, which is evidently a portrait, was the work of Hawkin of Liege and is of marble and not of alabaster. At the time of its erection it must have been one of the most sumptuous which the Abbey possessed. The tomb itself has been terribly mutilated. Of the seventy little figures which once adorned it, one alone remains complete, a charming little figure of a lady carrying a monkey on her arm. Queen Philippa's husband, Edward III (d. 1377), lies in the adjoining tomb. The effigy in bronze is perhaps by the craftsman who was responsible for the effigy of the Black Prince at Canterbury. The tomb is remarkable for the elaborately carved wooden canopy which surmounts it, and for the six little bronze figures of his children who appear as "weepers" on the side of the tomb towards the Ambulatory. Beneath them are beautifully executed enamelled shields of arms. Alabaster was used again for the curious little tomb of two of Edward III's children, William of Windsor and Blanche of the Tower, in St. Edmund's Chapel.

THE CHOIR. The site of the choir stalls, which occupy the three bays immediately west of the Crossing, has not been changed since the time of the Confessor. The 13th-century choir stalls were destroyed in 1775, the present ones being erected in 1834. In the Choir are sung the daily services when the Abbey choristers occupy the central part, and the clergy take their appointed places in canopied stalls. Over the pulpitum between Choir and Nave is the organ loft, of which only the stone core of the medieval work remains. The organ, originally by Schreider, was enlarged by Hill in 1884 and cased by Pearson in 1895.

43

Although they were babies when they died they are represented on their tomb as fully grown, but the figures themselves are less than two feet in length.

The finest and best preserved of the alabaster tombs in the Abbey is that to Simon Langham (d. 1376), sometime Abbot of Westminster, and afterwards Archbishop of Canterbury and a Cardinal. He is represented in mitre and mass-vestments, with crozier and pall. His feet rest upon two charming little pet-dogs with belled collars. Langham was a great benefactor to the Abbey, and it was due to him and to his successor as Abbot, Nicholas Litlyngton, that the great work of the rebuilding of the Nave was undertaken. It will be remembered that Henry III's work had ceased at the Choir and that the Nave of the Confessor's Church had been left standing, linked in some temporary way to the new work. In 1375 Litlyngton consulted Henry Yevele, the great medieval architect, and by a happy inspiration he decided that the new Nave should be continued after the pattern of the 13th-century work. A letter has been preserved among the Abbey muniments in which Litlyngton reports progress to the Cardinal, who was then in residence at Avignon. Writing on 1st April, 1376, he says "You must know that since Michaelmas there have been seven masons continually at work, and three at the Quarry at Reigate; and since Christmas ten masons to pull down the side of the old church next the cloister. And all is in readiness now for rising twelve feet in height and three pillars in length. I myself laid the first stone on the first Monday in Lent (3rd March, 1376) in honour of God and St. Peter."

For the next few years the work went rapidly ahead, and in it the King, Richard II, took the deepest personal interest. It is fitting that the portrait of the King as a young man, which he is believed to have himself given to the Abbey, should now hang in the Nave which owed much to his fostering care. Another contemporary painting, the large representation of Richard's badge of the chained White Hart, painted on the wall of the Muniment Room, may also have been his gift. Indeed, his benefactions of all kinds to the Abbey were on a princely scale. In 1394 he suffered a shattering blow in the death of the Queen, Anne of Bohemia. He immediately set about ordering a tomb for the Queen and himself to be erected within the Abbey. Yevele and Stephen Lote were commissioned to design an altar tomb "of pur marble" with six images on each side, and on it were to be placed gilt bronze effigies of the King and Queen lying hand-in-hand. The double tomb was an innovation and was to set a precedent for future Royal tombs. The tomb was completed and in place by 1399, and there was just time for the King himself to have seen it before he set out on his ill-fated expedition to Ireland which ultimately led to his deposition and subsequent murder. The effigies of the King and Queen were the work of Nicholas Broker and Godfrey Prest and, although sumptuous, are a little lacking in refinement. The robes of both, however, are powdered with very delicate pounce work representing their heraldic devices—the broompods, sunburst, couched hart, ostrich, etc.—interspersed with the crowned initials A and R and knots.

THE TOMB OF EDWARD III

The tomb of Edward III (*right*) which stands on the south side of the Confessor's Chapel, is one of the best preserved of Royal tombs of the 14th century. It was erected by his grandson and successor, Richard II, to the design of (probably) Henry Yevele, the great architect of the Nave. In niches on the face of the south side of the Purbeck-marble tomb are little gilt bronze "weepers" or mourners depicting (*from left to right in the photograph*) six of the King's children: the Black Prince; Joan de la Tour; Lionel, Duke of Clarence; Edmund, Duke of York; Mary, Duchess of Brittany; and William of Hatfield. There were once six other miniature effigies in the north side. At the base of the tomb are the Cross of St. George and the Arms of France and England on shields set in large quatrefoil panels.

THE EFFIGY

Upon the tomb of Edward III, on a brass plate, lies his gilt bronze effigy (*above, left*). It was executed by John Orchard in 1377 and is traditionally believed to have been modelled from a cast of the King's features made after death. The effigy, however, has formalised long hair and beard, and is vested in Coronation robes with Edward holding the shafts of two sceptres. Around the head is a recumbent canopy, also of brass, and above is a tester or canopy of oak, carved with panels and crockets. Quaint features of this piece of woodwork, not seen from ground level, are the humorous heads carved in obscure corners, examples of which are seen left.

Hitherto burial within the Abbey had been confined to members of the Royal Family and to those intimately connected with the Monastery. Under Richard II for the first time those who had stood high in his favour, such as John of Waltham, Bishop of Salisbury and Sir John Golofre, were accorded a like privilege. The innovation caused considerable indignation at the time, but it was one which was to grow steadily in the succeeding centuries.

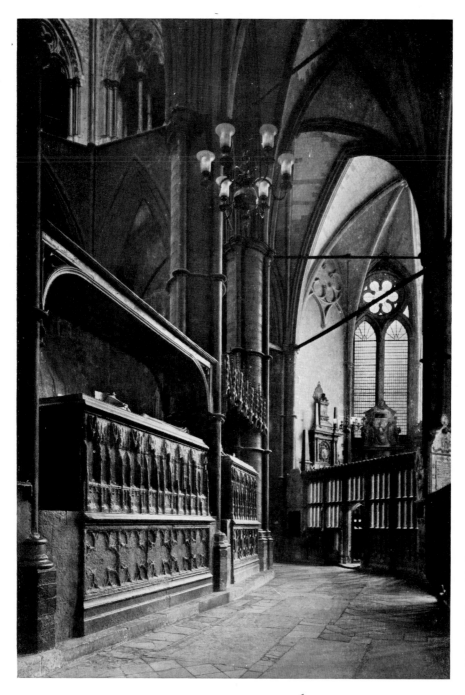

A view of the South Ambulatory showing on the left the tomb of Richard II and his Queen Consort, Anne of Bohemia, and that of Edward III. On the right of the photograph is seen the exterior of the Chapel of St. Nicholas.

Reproduced above is the seal of Thomas de Beauchamp, Earl of Warwick, an almost perfect impression in green wax. On the obverse is seen an equestrian figure bearing the Beauchamp arms on surcoat, shield and horse-trappings; the arms are a fess between six cross crosslets. The crest on the vizored helm is a swan's head proceeding from a coronet. On the reverse is a shield chequey, a chevron ermine for Warwick. The inscription on the obverse refers to Earl Thomas in a year of Edward III's reign which is specified on the reverse as being 1344. This is a fine example from the large collection of seals attached to documents in the Muniments of the Abbey. Such seals were used to certify letters and documents issued by nobles; the seal illustrated is attached to a lease.

*   *   *

THE LIBER REGALIS

This rare manuscript is a companion volume to the Litlyngton Missal (*see page* 95). In each is contained the text of the Royal Services, especially for Coronations; both are of the late 14th century and their wording is almost identical. Whereas the Missal, a large and heavy book, was written to be used at the High Altar, the Liber Regalis (size ten and a half by seven inches) was meant to be held in the hand. It is believed to have been so used by all Sovereigns from Henry IV to Elizabeth I. The manuscript is richly illuminated and contains four full-page minatures executed in gold and set off with blue, white and puce, each depicting a principal scene from the four Services. On the left of this page is shown the crowning of a king and, above, the crowning of a queen consort with a king. Provision is also made in the book for the separate Coronation of a queen consort, and also for the solemnity of a Royal funeral.

The late 14th-century Jerusalem Chamber (*above*) probably takes its name from the original tapestry which hung on its walls. This noble room is still adorned with tapestries, one of which is a 17th-century adaption of Raphael's cartoon of St. Peter healing a lame man at the Beautiful Gate. Other tapestries include a series showing the Life of Abraham, executed in Brussels about 1550. The timber roof, probably original, is supported by grotesquely carved corbels. The fireplace, of Tudor date, has a richly ornamented cedar wood overmantel added in the early 17th century. The Jerusalem Chamber, in which Henry IV died, is regularly used for meetings of the Dean and Chapter. Adjacent to it is the Jericho Parlour (*below, right*), part of the 16th-century Abbot's Lodgings. The Torrigiani medallion (*below, left*), is of Sir Thomas Lovell, Chancellor to Henry VII and Henry VIII.

5

THE CHANTRY CHAPEL OF HENRY V

THE 15th century opened gloomily for the monks of Westminster. The Monastery, which had for so long basked in Royal favour, was in disgrace for its loyalty to King Richard, and the Abbot was suspected of plotting against the new King. The work on the Nave more or less came to an end, and Henry IV seems deliberately to have transferred to Canterbury and to the rebuilding of the nave of that cathedral the interest and material assistance which his predecessors had given to Westminster. But retribution was to come. The wildness of the young Prince of Wales affected the King's health, and there were rumours that he had fallen a victim to the scourge of leprosy. Be that as it may, he was sufficiently well to come in March 1413 to pray at the Shrine of St. Edward in the Abbey. There he had a stroke. The terrified monks carried him through the half-finished Nave and laid him before the fire in the Jerusalem Chamber within the Abbot's Lodgings. He revived sufficiently to ask where he was. When they told him, even as we should today, that he was "in Jerusalem," he murmured, barely comprehending, that he would die happy for it had been foretold that death would come to him in the Holy Land. And so he passed away.

The scene, immortalised by Shakespeare, in which the young Prince tried on the Crown while his father lay senseless seems to rest on no foundation, but it is a fact that as soon as his father had died he went to the Abbey Anchorite or Recluse, John London, with whom he spent the night. Brother London had been a monk in the days of King Richard II and it may well be that he took the opportunity to draw the moral and to point out how the misfortunes of the late King's reign might be said to be due to his neglect of St. Edward and of the great work at the Abbey which King Richard had fostered. At any rate there is no doubt that within a few months the rebuilding of the Nave, from having been at a standstill, was again in full progress under Royal favour, and that the famous Richard Whittington, as an ex-Mayor and prominent citizen of London, was placed by the King in financial charge of the work. In the same year the King made further restitution by transferring the body of Richard II from Langley to the tomb at Westminster.

Nine years later the work on the Nave was temporarily suspended for the funeral of King Henry V himself. There are very full accounts of this pageant

49

of sombre and mournful splendour. On the coffin, we are told, lay the King's effigy clothed in his Royal robes. "The hatchments were borne only by captains to the number of twelve, and round about the chariot (on which the coffin rested) rode 500 men of arms all in black harness . . . with the butt of their spears upward . . . on every side of the chariot went 300 persons holding long torches, and Lords bearing banners, bannerets and pennons." The Abbey Sacrist's accounts, preserved among the Abbey Muniments, tell us that a way had been made "for bringing in horses into the Church," and thus the funeral chariot followed by the mourners and three armed knights on their chargers proceeded up the half-finished Nave to the entrance of the Choir, whence the coffin was borne to its resting place "with such solemn ceremonies, such mourning of lords, such prayer of priests, such lamenting of commons as never was before that day seen in the Realm of England."

The place for his tomb had been indicated by Henry himself in the will which he made in 1413. The circle of Royal tombs within the Confessor's Chapel was by then almost complete, but it was possible to find space by moving the Altar of the Holy Trinity and the Relic Chests, and by building out a platform into the Ambulatory. In the centre of this platform was placed the Purbeck-marble tomb of the King with a wooden effigy upon it covered originally with plates of silver gilt. It seems to have been in position by 1431. Just over a hundred years later, in 1546, it is recorded that thieves "had broken in the nyght season into the Churche of Westminster, and robbed away the Image of King Henry of Monmouth being all of sylver plates." All, therefore, that now remains on the tomb is the headless wooden core of the effigy.

Above the tomb is the King's Chantry Chapel, and this, too, was planned by Henry V himself. It spans the Ambulatory like a bridge and is reached by two turret stairways from the Confessor's Chapel. Henry seems to have had in mind the Tribune or raised platform from which relics were shown at the Sainte Chapelle in Paris. In the Chantry Chapel are cupboards or recesses intended for relics, while on the chestnut beam above are the Saddle—the earliest existing in England—the Helmet and the Shield which were carried at his funeral. The whole Chapel is covered with imagery and with carved representations of the King's badges—such as the Swan, the Beacon and the Antelope—and with his

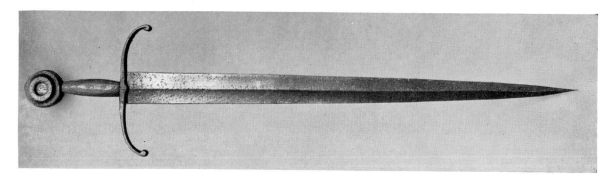

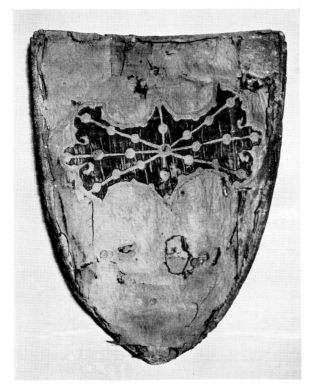

Part of the wall sculptures that adorn the Chantry Chapel of Henry V includes on the south-east side the fine equestrian figure seen below. It depicts Henry V in full armour on a caparisoned war-horse. The armour and horse-clothes are covered with the King's arms of France and England, and beneath is the Royal crest, a leopard surmounting a cap of estate on a helm. At the top of this page is seen the much worn silk embroidery on the reverse side of Henry V's shield.

HENRY V'S CHANTRY CHAPEL

The Chantry Chapel of Henry V, erected for the singing of masses for the souls of the dead King and his family, forms a bridge over the eastern Ambulatory and is reached by way of two newel staircases from the Confessor's Chapel. Above one end of the Chapel, by ancient custom, were placed the King's achievements on a wooden cross-beam (*above*). On the left is a saddle, in the centre a tilting helm and on the right a wooden shield covered with silk embroidery. It seems probable that the sword (*on facing page*), found in the triforium, was part of these achievements. In style it can be attributed to the early 15th century and is believed to be Henry V's own weapon. There are still traces of gilding on the iron blade, quillons and pommel, and in the sunken panels of the pommel are red crosses on a gold ground. There is no evidence that these objects were used by Henry V at Agincourt though this is popularly supposed. In a turret of the Chantry Chapel was found a cloth-yard shaft or arrow for a longbow which has a metal point, clearly of the type used at that historic battle.

coat of arms. On the sides above the Ambulatory are carved scenes representing the King's Coronation, and representations of the King on horseback in full armour. The work on the Chantry Chapel was carried out by John Thirske, the Master Mason in charge of the rebuilding of the Nave, and it seems to have been completed by about 1450.

Close to the King's tomb is the fine tomb of his standard bearer at Agincourt, Lewis Robsart, Lord Bourchier, who died in 1431. It cannot be doubted that the position was deliberately chosen. The tomb is ingeniously contrived to form an integral part of the Screen to the Chapel of St. Paul. It must have been of great splendour, but only faint traces now remain of the blaze of heraldry which was formerly painted on the stonework. Flanking the canopy of the tomb are carved stone banners bearing the Bourchier coat of arms supported by large heraldic falcons and lions—a striking and unusual feature.

The Chantry Chapel of King Henry V was a notable addition to the Abbey Church. The deeply worn steps in the turrets which lead up to it show that it was used daily not only by those whose duty it was to say masses for the King's soul, but by the monk who was in charge of the Shrine with its relics and treasures. A somewhat similar "watching chamber" may be seen near the Shrine in St. Alban's Abbey Church.

While the Chantry Chapel was building, Thirske and his craftsmen were also engaged in erecting the stone Screen at the western end of the Confessor's Chapel which also forms the back of the High Altar. This Screen, with its two doors on either side of the Altar, was finished in 1441. On the Altar side the Screen has been ruthlessly modernised, but on the Shrine side the original work remains although it has been much defaced. In the cove of the cornice is an interesting series of fourteen little carved scenes representing incidents in the life of the Confessor. Above the screen was placed originally a triptych flanked by figures of St. Peter and St. Paul. Above these again was the Rood Beam with its Crucifix and figures of the Virgin Mary and St. John and attendant Seraphim. All this towering superstructure was swept away at the Reformation.

This great Screen materially altered the appearance of the eastern end of Henry III's Church. Not only did it hide the Shrine from the Choir, but it cut right across the surrounding circle of Royal tombs which had hitherto extended to the steps leading to the Altar. Something like the original arrangement at Westminster can still be seen at Canterbury where, although the Shrine of Becket has disappeared, the uninterrupted view from the Choir enhances the beauty of the Apse. Certainly the pre-15th-century view of the east end of Westminster, with the great gold Shrine in the centre rising above Abbot Ware's pavement and the Altar, and surrounded with the Royal tombs, must have been one of almost unimaginable splendour.

The troubled reign of King Henry VI left little mark at Westminster. He himself had wished to be buried there with his ancestors, and the record remains among the Abbey Muniments of a visit which he paid in order to choose a site

THE CHANTRY CHAPEL OF HENRY V, built over the Ambulatory between the Chapel of the Kings and Henry VII's Chapel, is adorned with sculptures of the early 15th century. Set above a display of Royal arms and crests on this, the south side, is a scene from the Coronation of Henry V. Supported by two bishops and seated crowned on his throne, he is depicted holding the Orb and Sceptre. On either side stand hooded lords. In the shadow (*see page* 51) is a fine equestrian figure of the King in full armour.

for his future tomb.   When the Abbot suggested a place by the side of his father, Henry V, the King replied, "Nay, let him alone, he lieth like a noble prince, I will not trouble him."   Eventually a place was chosen between the Shrine and the tomb of Henry III, and the King ordered Thirske, who was in attendance, to mark it out there and then with his pickaxe.   Fate eventually decided that Henry should be buried elsewhere, but the outline traced by Thirske still remains on the floor of the Chapel—a silent witness to his unfulfilled wish.

The close of the century was the threshold of a new age, and it was marked at Westminster by the fact that in 1476 William Caxton set up the first printing press in England in a small shop which stood near the Lady Chapel and the Chapter House of the Abbey, and within a few yards of the house where the poet, Geoffrey Chaucer, had died seventy-six years before.   A few years later, in 1483, as his trade increased, Caxton took in addition to the original shop the rather larger premises known as the Red Pale within the Abbey Almonry.   The fact that his shops were close to and possibly abutted upon the Lady Chapel and also upon the little Chapel of St. Anne within the Almonry has resulted, perhaps, in the use to this day of the word "Chapel" to denote an association of printers.

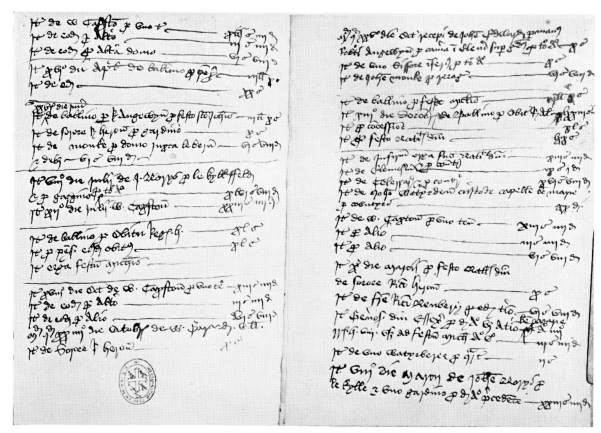

The page of the Sub Prior's Rent Book recording William Caxton's payments for the years 1482 to 1491 for three tenements and a chamber over the way to the Almonry.   He first took rooms in the precincts at Michaelmas, 1476, and in the following year his English edition of *The Dictes or Sayengis of the Philosophres* was issued.

54

A BESTIARY

This beast book is included among the medieval manuscripts in the Abbey Library. It is a most curious volume of moralising tales, the themes of which are comparable with Æsop's fables. Every page has hand-coloured illustrations of animals and mythical monsters more or less realistically depicted, and the stories are traceable to the 8th century. The Abbey copy is of early 13th-century date written on vellum in England. The photograph (*right*) shows a full-page illustration of the famous Elephant and Castle. Elephants were known in England in the 13th century, but it is questionable whether the artist had ever seen one. In the formidable castle strapped upon the elephant's back are soldiers in chain mail, and on the topmost turret of the castle one is actually firing a cross-bow. Perhaps it is from this illustration that the tavern sign, the Elephant and Castle, is derived.

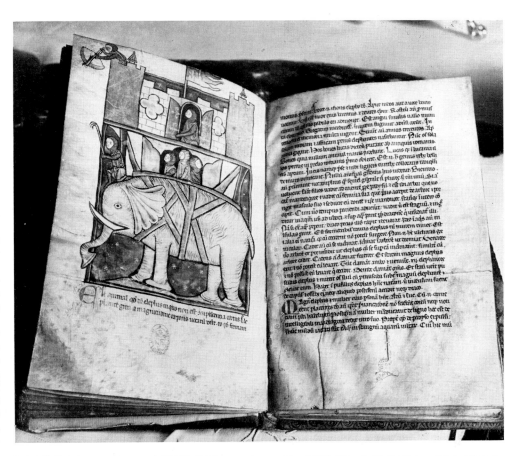

CHAUCER'S LEASE

This document (*above*) is from the great collection of archives of the Abbey. It is of particular interest as it is the last undoubted reference to Geoffrey Chaucer, the poet, in his lifetime. By this lease he is granted a tenement in the Abbey precincts at the side of the old Lady Chapel that formerly stood on the site of Henry VII's Chapel. It is dated A.D. 1399 in the reign of Henry IV, with the assent of William of Colchester, the Abbot. Chaucer is known to have died the following year, so he did not enjoy the property for more than a few months. The tenement was demolished at the beginning of the 16th-century to make way for the building of Henry VII's Chapel.

In recent years there were found in the binding of a kitchen account book of the Abbey several pages of books and five playing cards (*left*) as padding. This account book was first used in 1521, and it must therefore have been bound before that date. These, then, are in all probability, the oldest playing cards in England.

HENRY VII'S CHAPEL. This marvel of perpendicular architecture is in considerable contrast to the rest of the Abbey Church. It is probably one of the most ornate and splendid Royal chapels. The walls are adorned with nearly a hundred statuettes in niches, the fan vaulting of the roof is an incredible study in stone con-struction. Henry VII's Chapel contains his tomb and the graves of many other Kings and Queens. The original altar was destroyed in 1643 though some fragments of it were incorporated in the reproduction now seen. In this superb setting Knights of the Most Honourable Order of the Bath are installed.

THE ADORNMENT OF HENRY VII'S CHAPEL

On this page can be seen certain of the details of the decoration and adornment of Henry VII's Chapel and his tomb. The stone panelling of the Chapel walls is relieved throughout by carved figures of a heraldic and symbolic nature. Over the doorways are quatrefoils filled with fleurs-de-lys, and above is a frieze of carved winged angels with arms half-raised between crowned Tudor double roses, crowned yales and the heraldic portcullises of the Beaufort family, from whom the King was descended in the female line. This frieze continues round the whole of the Chapel; on other walls these same motifs appear together with carved beasts and Royal coats-of-arms. The great bronze-plated oak gates (right) are richly decorated with the crowned yale, the leopards of England, the King's monogram, "HR," the falcon and fetterlock, the triple fleur-de-lys of France, the root of daisies and the thorn-bush. All these symbols are Royal badges, and some of them are reproduced above. The font of Purbeck marble is of the 15th century but has been much restored. At the western end of the Chapel are the stalls of the Sovereign and of the Great Master of the Order of the Bath. On the right of this page is a view of two of the very graceful bronze cherubs that adorn each corner of the tomb of Henry VII and support the Royal Coat of Arms surrounded by the Garter. An inscription, in Latin, in praise of Henry VII and his Queen Consort, Elizabeth of York, who is buried with him, passes round the four sides of the upper part of the tomb. The black marble tomb has a beautifully carved frieze and is adorned with medallions in bronze-gilt, representing the Virgin and Henry's ten patron saints. A small altar (where relics such as the leg of St. George and a piece of the true Cross were kept) used to stand at the foot of the tomb. The ornate grille which surrounds the tomb, may be seen on page 61.

FAN VAULTING : ROYAL TOMBS

In the Nave of Henry VII's Chapel the bold, coloured banners of the Knights Grand Cross of the Most Honourable Order of the Bath contrast vividly with the delicate tracery of the fan-vaulted ceiling and enhance its beauty. At each new Investiture, banners of deceased knights are taken down to be returned to their families and replaced by those of newly installed members. In the North Aisle of the Chapel, the principal tomb is that of the two half-sisters, Mary Tudor and Elizabeth I (*left*). On this white marble tomb erected by James I in 1606, Elizabeth's recumbent effigy is notable for its resemblance to her later portraits. Inserted in the tomb is a gold ring with a sardonyx cameo portrait of the Queen, given by her according to tradition to the Earl of Essex. Beneath Elizabeth's coffin lies that of Mary Tudor. At the eastern end of this same Chapel, often called Innocent's Corner, is the tomb of Princess Sophia, (*above, left*) a daughter of James I who died in 1606 aged two days. She is represented as lying in a cradle "wherewith vulgar eyes, especially of the weaker sex, are more affected (as level to their cognisance more capable of what is pretty than what is pompous) than all the magnificent monuments in Westminster." This pathetic little tomb, on a black marble step, is a rocking cradle with a richly ornamented hood of alabaster, containing the life-like figure of a baby beautifully carved in the same material.

6

A GREAT KING AND A GREAT ABBOT

"ON entering Henry VII's Chapel the eye is astonished by the pomp of architecture, and the elaborate beauty of sculptured detail. The very walls are wrought into universal ornament, incrusted with tracery and scooped into niches, crowded with the statues of saints and martyrs. Stone seems, by the cunning labour of the chisel, to have been robbed of its weight and density, suspended aloft, as if by magic, and the fretted roof achieved with the wonderful minuteness and airy security of a cobweb." In these words Washington Irving, in his *Sketchbook*, describes the Chapel which Francis Bacon, just two centuries earlier, had called the stateliest and daintiest in Europe. And, indeed, from the time of its completion it has never failed to excite admiration. Begun in 1503, Henry VII originally intended it to be the resting place of Henry VI, but that project was eventually given up and the Chapel became his own Mausoleum and most enduring monument.

The actual accounts for the building have never come to light, but it is fairly certain that the architect was Robert Vertue assisted by his brother William Vertue. To them must be attributed the astonishingly daring and beautiful vaulting of the Chapel. Nothing was spared to make the Chapel, as the late Professor Lethaby called it, "one of the most perfect buildings ever erected in England." The richness of the carved work of the Stalls, the painted windows, destroyed indeed in Cromwellian times, but which Barnard Flower, the King's Glazier, was ordered to take as his pattern for the still existing windows of King's College Chapel, Cambridge, the bronze entrance gates and the unique series of carved stone saints which surround the Chapel at the triforium level, must have made the interior, when it was first built, one of marvellous beauty.

It is curious that just as Italian craftsmen had been called in to make the Shrine of the Confessor in the 13th century, so now the Italian, Torrigiani, was commissioned to design the tomb of Henry VII and Elizabeth of York. This great Renaissance tomb, which stands behind the High Altar, was made between 1512 and 1518–19. It superseded an earlier design by Paganino of which the bronze grille or screen by Thomas Ducheman, which still surrounds the tomb, is probably a survival. The design of the present tomb, with its charming little bronze cherubs seated on the corners of the entablature, is purely Italian. Two

59

other works of Torrigiani are also within the Chapel. The beautiful tomb of the King's mother, the Lady Margaret, Countess of Richmond (d. 1509), is in the South Aisle. The contract for making it is dated 1511 and it seems to have been completed in 1514. Dean Stanley called it "the most beautiful and venerable figure which the Abbey contains." Nearby hangs the bronze medallion of Sir Thomas Lovell (d. 1524), sometime Speaker of the House of Commons. This also is the work of Torrigiani. It was for many years preserved at Lovell's former home, East Harling Manor, Norfolk, but was eventually given to the Abbey in 1902.

Another of Henry VII's trusted friends, Giles, Lord Daubeny (d. 1507), lies buried in St. Paul's Chapel near the entry to Henry VII's Chapel. He had desired to be buried as near as possible to the new Chapel which Henry VII was then erecting. The tomb, with its alabaster effigies of himself and his wife, has been over-restored, but it is a characteristic example of its type. Its most interesting feature consists of the two little figures of bedesmen carved on the soles of Lord Daubeny's shoes.

The first quarter of the 16th century saw the completion not only of Henry VII's Chapel but of the rebuilding of the Nave. Throughout this period the last of the great Abbots of Westminster, John Islip, held sway over the Monastery. He was in many ways a remarkable man, and it was certainly due to him that the Nave was finally completed. It had taken the best part of a hundred and fifty years to rebuild, but even as the last stones were being placed in position fresh work was undertaken and Islip was among those who assisted in laying the foundation stone of the King's new Chapel. Before his death he was to see the completion of this Chapel too. Nor was this all the building connected with his name. During his lifetime he seems to have built the Chantry Chapel in the North Ambulatory in which he was ultimately to be buried. This two-storied structure, known in his day as "the Jesus Chapel beneath and the Jesus Chapel above," has carved upon it the Abbot's rebus, an eye and a tree with a hand plucking off a branch or slip and a man slipping from a tree. He had also added to the Abbot's lodging the Jericho Parlour, with its linenfold panelling, and the adjoining rooms, together with the gallery looking down into the Nave known today as the Abbot's Pew.

As the Abbot's long life drew to its close he must have been conscious of the gathering clouds. He had seen the rise of Wolsey. As Abbot he had taken his part in the solemn service at the Abbey when the Cardinal's hat had been placed on Wolsey's head. He lived just long enough to see his fall. It had been given to him to see his Abbey Church complete, as never before or since, with all the beauty of its colour, its imagery, its glass and its paintings undefaced. When he died in 1532 the end of medieval monasticism was in sight. The Abbot's Mortuary Roll, with its precious contemporary pen and ink drawings showing among others his Chantry Chapel and the scene at the High Altar at his funeral, is among the treasures of the Abbey Muniment Room. They are the only

THE TOMB OF HENRY VII is the work of Pietro Torrigiani, a contemporary of Michelangelo, and is the earliest of its kind in England, since it was begun in 1512 and finished about 1518. On the tomb rest superb bronze effigies of the King and his Queen, Elizabeth of York; the magnificent bronze grille that surrounds the tomb—a 16th-century masterpiece—is by Thomas Ducheman.

medieval drawings of the interior of the Abbey which are known to exist. The fine contemporary carved stone head of an Abbot, now in the Library, with its austere but strongly marked personality, is almost certainly a portrait of Abbot Islip.

In 1540, eight years after Islip's death, the Monastery was dissolved, and for a few years the Abbey became a Cathedral under the first and last Bishop of Westminster, Thomas Thirleby. The last Abbot became the first Dean, and the Prior and some of the monks were numbered among the new Prebendaries. An inventory was made of the plate, vestments and other treasures of the dissolved Monastery, and almost all these things passed into the hands of King Henry VIII or others. The devastation and spoliation became complete under Edward VI. By the accession of Queen Mary I in 1553 St. Katherine's Chapel in the Infirmary, the Refectory and other monastic buildings had been pulled down and the Church itself had been ruthlessly "cleansed" of what were termed "monuments of idolatry and superstition."

In 1556 the Queen determined to restore the Monastery. Over thirty ex-monks were collected from former monasteries and placed under the care of John Feckenham as Abbot. Feckenham himself had formerly been a monk at Evesham and, after spending most of the reign of Edward VI in prison as a Papist, had recently been made Dean of St. Paul's. He was a man of outstanding ability with few personal enemies, and an excellent preacher. But the re-establishment of the Monastery was foredoomed to failure. It could not be otherwise than a makeshift affair, and the precarious health of the Queen must have made it obvious that the community could look for no abiding habitation at Westminster. Feckenham did what he could. The Shrine of the Confessor was repaired and the existing wooden superstructure took the place of the gold feretory which had been plundered; the old right of sanctuary was re-established and as far as was possible the monastic routine was restored. In November 1558, however, the Queen died, and although Feckenham and his monks played their part at the Coronation of her successor the Monastery was again dissolved a few months later.

ABBOT ISLIP

John Islip was the last of the great medieval Abbots. Though he died in 1532, eight years before the Dissolution of the Abbey, he had to meet many encroachments on his authority, but nevertheless his period of office was memorable. He himself laid the foundation stone of Henry VII's Chapel, saw the completion of the Nave and the glazing of the great West Window, and superintended the erection of the Western Towers to the height of the roof, and many smaller works were undertaken in his time. A favourite of two kings, Henry VII and Henry VIII, he was a Privy Counsellor as well as Abbot of Westminster, and his funeral was an occasion of almost Royal pomp. His Mortuary Roll, still preserved in the Abbey, depicts in beautiful outline drawings attributed to Holbein, several scenes of the funeral. These include impressions of the Abbot's deathbed, his tomb in the Islip Chapel and the hearse at his funeral service. The drawing of the hearse (*right*) is notable for its architectural details and for showing the Great Rood that stood over the High Altar. Islip's hearse is surmounted by a forest of candelabra, and is decorated with coats of arms and the Rebus of Islip. Around it are the monks of Westminster. The Rebus (*below, left*) is a pun on Islip's name; an eye with a slip or branch and a boy slipping from a tree. The impressive early 16th-century head carved in stone (*below, right*), found embedded in masonry at the restoration of the North Transept, is possibly the only surviving likeness of this great Abbot.

The exterior of Henry VII's Chapel was entirely refaced in 1807 by James Wyatt, later called the "Destroyer" for the ruthlessness of his restoration work. The Chapel had been much neglected, and in 1803 the outside was said to be "almost a shapeless mass of ruins." Wyatt left nothing of the original facings. The remains of Tudor carvings were removed and in part replaced, but with no inspiration or feeling for the beautiful 16th-century work. On the left is seen the charming little wooden figure of a king robed and crowned, standing on the stall of the Great Master of the Order of the Bath in Henry VII's Chapel, and below is the striking gilt bronze effigy of Henry VII on his tomb. It was executed by Pietro Torrigiani, and is undoubtedly a portrait, probably taken from a death-mask of the King.

7

THE ELIZABETHAN FOUNDATION

THE accession of Queen Elizabeth I opened a new chapter in the history of Westminster Abbey. The uncertainties of the preceding twenty years came to an end. The attempts to replace the medieval Monastery, first by a Cathedral establishment under a Bishop in the reign of Henry VIII and then by a restored Monastery in the reign of Queen Mary, had both proved to be failures. The new Collegiate Church of St. Peter in Westminster, founded by Queen Elizabeth in 1560 with a Dean at its head, on the other hand, has lasted from that date to the present day. In itself the new foundation differed but little from that of Henry VIII, but the absence of a Bishop meant that it depended more directly upon the Queen herself, and from the first she took a personal interest in it. Nor was it to be an exclusively ecclesiastical body. In the foundation charter emphasis was laid upon education in order that "youth, who in the stock of our republic, like certain tender twigs, daily increase, may be liberally trained up in useful letters, to the greater ornament of the same republic." For this reason the School within the precincts, which had existed as a grammar school since the 14th century, was brought into greater prominence and definitely connected by scholarships both with Trinity College, Cambridge, and with Christ Church, Oxford. In this way the Queen became in a very real sense its Foundress.

It was a curious inheritance upon which the new Dean and his Prebendaries entered; "a mighty skeleton" as Dean Stanley called it "which was to be slowly reanimated with a new life." The Church itself was intact, but stripped of its many altars and much of its internal fittings it must have looked curiously bare, and was cruelly scarred by the marks left by those who had carried out all too faithfully the work of removing traces of "superstition." It requires an effort to remember that in 1561 there were not more than about thirty actual tombs within the Church, and that these were all within the circle of Chapels at its eastern end. The Nave, the Choir and its Aisles, and the Transepts were completely bare of monuments. There was one exception. In 1556 Nicholas Brigham, himself a minor poet, who was then living within the Precincts, placed a monument to Chaucer in the east aisle of the South Transept. It is often said that this monument was a second-hand one which Brigham was content to pick up cheap and re-use for the purpose. But it is in fact of a type which came into existence in the second half of the 15th century and persisted far into the 16th century. It can be paralleled, for instance, by the tomb of Sir William Fitz-williams (d. 1551) at Windsor, and it forms one of a group which preserved the old Gothic tradition, little affected by the influence of the Renaissance.

This solitary tomb, looking back to a former age, was in fact to gather round it the poets and writers of later ages in a "Poets' Corner," just as in the future the statesmen were to gather in the North Transept, the soldiers and sailors in the Nave, and the men of science, art and music in the north Choir Aisle. It was indeed the opening of the doors of the Abbey not only to public worship but to every kind of monument and memorial tablet which was to be the outstanding feature of the Elizabethan and succeeding ages.

With the new foundation the great age of building at Westminster came to an end. In the Middle Ages the Monastery was never free from scaffolding and work-men engaged either on the rebuilding of the Nave or, at the beginning of the 16th century, on Henry VII's Chapel. But from 1561 no addition was made to the fabric of the Church for nearly two hundred years, and the only problem, and it was a very real one, was how to keep it in repair. There was, however, much rebuilding within the precincts. The ruined monastic buildings were either rebuilt or adapted to the needs of the School and the Prebends, and those which were not required for Collegiate purposes were leased to those who found it con-venient to live within easy distance of the Palace and the Houses of Parliament.

It was partly due to this last fact that in the last decades of the 16th century the Abbey began to be filled with the towering monuments of the Elizabethan magnates. No fewer than eleven of these were erected between 1580 and 1601. Hitherto the tombs in the Abbey had stood separate and detached in their respective Chapels. Some of these later 16th-century tombs followed this earlier and simpler tradition, but others monumental in every sense of the word, and mostly erected to the memory of the great ladies of the Court of Queen Elizabeth I, were so designed that they had perforce to be fixed for support against the walls of the Church. As their height would have obscured the windows many of them occupy the site of the former altars, which were usually placed against windowless walls in the side Chapels.

The simple and dignified tombs of the Elizabethan soldiers, William Thynne and Sir Francis Vere,[1] contrast with such enormous monuments as those to Mildred, the second wife of the great Lord Burghley; Frances, Countess of Sussex (the Foundress of Sidney Sussex College, Cambridge); Henry Carey, Lord Hunsdon (whose monument is no less than 36 feet high); and Henry, Lord Norris. This last monument, with its pillared canopy, is remarkable for the six life-sized figures in armour representing the six Norris sons, who kneel round their parents. Four of these sons fell in battle, one alone survived his father and

---

[1] Mr. A. J. Taylor, F.S.A., has drawn my attention to the hitherto unnoticed fact that this tomb in its general design is a close copy of the tomb at Breda erected to Earl Engelbrecht II van Nassau (d. 1504).

Geoffrey Chaucer's tomb (*below, right*) was erected by Nicholas Brigham in 1556 out of his respect for this great medieval poet, and round the spot were later to be gathered the tombs and memorials in what is now known as Poets' Corner. Above may be seen 19th-century memorials to Thomas Campbell, Samuel Taylor Coleridge, Southey, Dr. Johnson, Shakespeare, Burns and James Thomson. On the wall (*right of the photograph*) are two of the most important surviving 13th-century wall paintings in England. They represent the Incredulity of St. Thomas, and St. Christopher bearing Christ through the Waters of Life.

There is a legend that the initials "I.W." on the monument of Isaac Casaubon (*above*) are those of Izaak Walton, author of *The Compleat Angler*. It is said that, determined to be represented in Poets' Corner, he scratched them himself!

brothers and so "while the rest are represented praying and with bowed heads he looks cheerfully upward." They are very striking figures and give immense dignity to the tomb.

For Queen Elizabeth, her successor James I erected a detached tomb in the north aisle of Henry VII's Chapel. It was designed by Cornelius Cure, and his original coloured sketch for the tomb is now in the Bibliotheque Nationale, Paris. The effigy on the tomb was the work of Maximilian Colt, and, perhaps more than any of the pictures of the Queen, suggests her outstanding personality. It had been the Queen's intention to erect somewhat similar tombs for her predecessors, Queen Mary and King Edward VI. A design for the tomb of Edward VI, perhaps also by Cure, exists in the Bodleian at Oxford.[1] But for some reason these projects were never carried out, and while Edward rests beneath the altar in Henry VII's Chapel, Mary shares the same vault with her sister Elizabeth. "Consorts both in throne and grave, here sleep the two sisters, Elizabeth and Mary, in the hope of one resurrection." So runs the Latin epitaph on their tomb, and, as Dean Stanley wrote, "the long war of the English Reformation is closed in these words. In that contracted sepulchre, admitting of none other than those two, the stately coffin of Elizabeth rests on the coffin of Mary. The sisters are at one: the daughter of Catherine of Arragon and the daughter of Anne Boleyn repose in peace at last."

In the corresponding aisle on the south side of Henry VII's Chapel James I erected another stately tomb to the memory of his own mother, Mary, Queen of Scots, whose body he caused to be removed from Peterborough to Westminster in 1612. It is a curious fact that with the tombs of the two rival Queens the long series of Royal monuments at Westminster came to an end. James I, Charles II, Mary II, William III, Anne and George II all lie buried within Henry VII's Chapel, but no monuments were erected over their graves. Designs were made for tombs for some of them, but they were never carried out and their names cut in the pavement are their only memorial.

The costly tombs of the courtiers and others of the reigns of James I and Charles II continued to be erected, like those of the Elizabethans, until the outbreak of the Civil War. But no further Royal tombs were erected except the enchanting little monuments to James I's two infant children at the east end of the north aisle of Henry VII's Chapel. Maximilian Colt designed these monuments, and with charming simplicity the little Princess Sophia sleeps in her stone cradle—"a royal rosebud, untimely plucked by death; torn from her parents to bloom afresh in the rosegarden of Christ"—while the Princess Mary, who lived to the age of two and a half years, dressed in stomacher, Medici collar and French cap, reclines stiffly on her left arm.

It has seemed worthwhile to draw attention to this large group of Elizabethan and early 17th-century monuments. Altogether there are some thirty or more of them, and no other church has so large and varied a collection. Unless,

[1] H. M. Colvin *Architectural Drawings in the Bodleian Library, Pl.* 1.

TUDOR HERALDRY

The Chapel of Henry VII is a memorial not only to its founder but to his family, the House of Tudor, as well. The display of heraldic devices pertaining to the House, so evident in every corner of the Chapel, is perhaps unparalled elsewhere in variety and beauty, and symbolises each of the Royal lines joined in the marriage of Henry Tudor to Elizabeth of York, and also the conclusion of the Wars of the Roses. The Tudor roses appear as a complement to the other badges: the yale or portcullis of the Beauforts, the house of Henry VII's mother; her root of daisies; the falcon and fetterlock of York; the collar of SS-knots and broompods of Lancaster, and the crowned fleur-de-lys. The supporters are beasts including the dragon of Cadwallader, the greyhound of the Nevilles, the lions of England and the antelope of the Beauforts, a statuette of which is seen below.

THE BATTLE OF BRITAIN CHAPEL

The extreme eastern side-chapel in Henry VII's Chapel was dedicated in 1947 to the memory of the officers and men of the Royal Air Force killed in the Battle of Britain. The principal part of the memorial is a stained-glass window, designed and made by Mr. Hugh Easton, the lower lights of which contain the badges of the sixty-three Fighter Squadrons that took part in the Battle. In four panels are visions symbolising the Redemption, with the Heavenly Seraphim above, arms outstretched. Below the window in the wall is preserved a hole made by a piece of shrapnel during the Battle which was fought over London and the Home Counties in the late summer of 1940. The altar, designed by Professor A. E. Richardson, R.A., is of English walnut; the silver gilt Cross and candelabra and the silver altar rails, designed by Mr. J. Seymour Lindsay, are described later in this book. In the adjoining chapel is a Roll of Honour inscribed with the names of those who died. The wall niches contain two of the 95 remaining stone statuettes, 107 of which originally adorned Henry VII's Chapel. The nearer, representing St. Nicholas, is of a bishop with a crozier and a boy in a basket in his left hand; the other, depicting St. Thomas of Canterbury, is of an archbishop with a cross-staff and an open book.

however, an attempt is made to visualise them as a whole and as they would have appeared before the outbreak of the Civil War in 1642, they tend to become isolated and overwhelmed owing to the multitude of monuments and tablets of a later age by which they have come to be surrounded. When they were first erected they must have added colour and warmth to a rather bare church. The worst that can be said of them is that they probably hide remains of earlier work which would be better appreciated now than at that time, and that in some instances arcading was ruthlessly cut away in order to fit them into their places. But in themselves these great tombs with their coloured marbles, their obelisks, their wealth of heraldry and their dignified recumbent effigies are not unworthy of their setting. They express exactly the spirit of their age, and they deserve a closer and more appreciative study than is sometimes accorded to them.

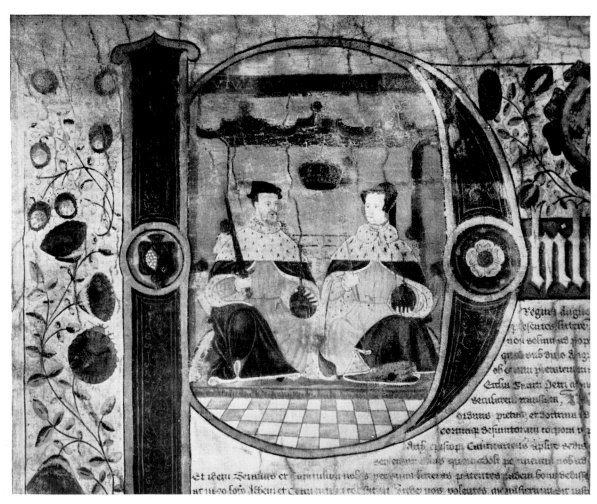

A charter of many pages issued by Mary Tudor, in an endeavour to re-establish the Abbey of Westminster, is prefaced by this illuminated picture of the Queen and her husband, Philip of Spain. Mary holds the orb and a sceptre, Philip holds an orb and a sword; the Crown of England is placed between them.

HENRY VII CHAPEL INDENTURES

Still preserved in the Abbey are several magnificent copies of the indenture or bond drawn up in 1504 between Abbot Islip and the Convent of Westminster and Henry VII. Therein is written the full intentions of the King for the maintenance of his new Chapel and instructions regarding the Services to be conducted there in perpetuity. A number of witnesses guaranteed that the King's directions would be carried out, each having a copy of the bond to which their seals were attached. These seals, are preserved in small metal boxes attached by silken cords, and the bindings are of blue velvet embossed with Tudor roses and portcullises (*below, left*). The page of introduction (*left*) is illuminated and the text is written in English and Latin. At the top of this page is seen the signature of Henry VIII. Below, right, is an illuminated initial on a charter of the same King, founding the short-lived See and Cathedral of Westminster in place of the Abbey he dissolved.

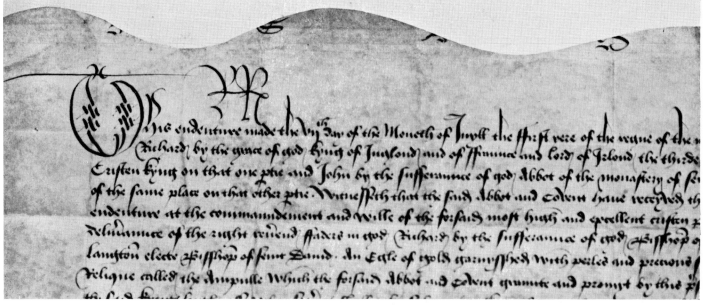

SOME MUNIMENTS

The three small sections of early 13th-century documents at the top of the page are of interest as the writers have endeavoured to introduce a note of humour by drawing curious heads into the initial letters. The document in the centre has particular significance to the history of the Coronation Regalia, since it carries mention of "An Eagle of gold garnysshed with perles and precious stones . . . the relique called the Ampulla . . . in the custody of the Abbot and Convent of Westminster." Though the Ampulla now used for containing the Holy Oil for the anointing ritual shows no trace of jewels, it is very probably the relic referred to, somewhat refashioned at the Restoration after having survived the general destruction of the Regalia. This document, written in English, is endorsed with the sign-manual of Richard III. The magnificent 12th-century, iron-bound oak chest (right), over 12 feet long, still holds documents from the Muniments as it did in the Middle Ages.

THE ABBEY LIBRARY. This was formerly part of the Monks' Dorter, or Dormitory, built about 1300; re-roofed, it is said, in the late 15th century. Through the end wall is a passage leading to the 'night-stairs' by which the monks went to attend night services in the church. In 1623 Dean Williams had the present bookcases erected. The Library now contains some 12,000 books.

THE ROYAL FUNERAL EFFIGIES

The funeral effigies of medieval kings and queens were authentic likenesses made to lie in state above the coffined bodies in costly hearses blazing with light. The earliest existing effigy is of 14th-century date. Some of the heads are death masks in plaster; others were carved in wood from such masks, but all the effigies were painted to be lifelike and Royally robed, crowned and sceptred. Restoration by Mr. R. P. Howgrave-Graham has revealed that the oldest head, that of Edward III (d. 1377), is a death mask and the earliest one known of European origin. The face (*bottom, right*) shows the paralysis due to the fatal stroke which deprived him of speech. The two women's heads are carved portraits of Anne of Bohemia, Queen of Richard II (d. 1394), and Elizabeth of York, Queen of Henry VII (d. 1503), whose beautiful carved hand before her carries material which before restoration was stiff with grey dirt until washing revealed it to be of exquisite satin. Anne's head was carved from a death mask. The pathetic effigy of Katherine de Valois, the Queen of Henry V and the "Dear Kate" of Shakespeare's play, suggests the tragedy of her end. The head (*below, centre*) is ringed to take the crown. The splendid and important death mask of Henry VII (*below, left*) shows on the right eyebrow, the clotting of hair due to grease applied when taking the mould.

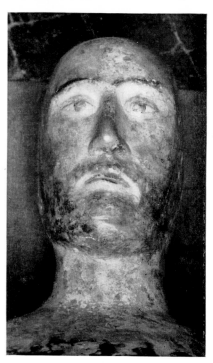

8

THE NATION'S CHURCH

IN the preceding chapters some attempt has been made to suggest that it is worth-while to study the growth of the Abbey by periods, and by drawing attention to some of the principal additions both to the fabric and to the "furnishings" (i.e. tombs, painting, sculpture, etc.) in any particular century to try to see the Abbey as it would have appeared to those living at the time. This is the easier to do in the Middle Ages because, while we must never forget the daily routine of prayer, praise and work within the Monastery, the monks and their Royal and other benefactors were continually employing skilled craftsmen to build or rebuild or otherwise add to the Church and its contents.

But except for the fact that the Abbey Church was the Coronation Church and the burial place of kings, and that the House of Commons frequently met within its Chapter House or its Refectory, the concerns of the Monastery were essentially self-centred, and the monks for the most part led, as indeed was fitting, a life apart. Speaking generally Westminster Abbey, except as one of the greater Benedictine Abbeys, meant little to the ordinary citizen, even of Westminster. Except on business he rarely, if ever, entered even its outer precinct, and its services, its ordered routine and all that was of absorbing interest to the monks themselves were of little or no concern to him in his daily life. The rebuilding of the parish church of St. Margaret about 1500 was of far greater interest to him, and affected him much more closely, than the rebuilding of the Nave of the Abbey Church or of the King's new Chapel at about the same time.

But with the passing of the Monastery and the subsequent foundation of the Collegiate Church all this changed. Slowly, but inevitably, through its daily services, its music, its preaching, its Royal and other services on great occasions, its ever-growing number of memorials and through its historic associations the "mighty skeleton," to use Stanley's phrase, became clothed with flesh and was reanimated. It was no longer merely the Church of a Benedictine Abbey but a Church which was open to all who wished to join in its services and in its worship. In the centuries which followed it gradually became a national shrine, ever increasingly regarded with a kind of personal affection by English-speaking peoples throughout the world. And as this feeling grew, so too there came, slowly and through curious variations of taste, an appreciation of the beauty of the building itself, both as a whole and in all its parts, demanding reverence and care in its preservation and in any addition either to its fabric or to its internal adornment.

In striking contrast, therefore, to earlier ages the history of the Abbey since Elizabethan times has been concerned less with construction in a material sense than with the gradual building up of a new conception of the meaning of this great Church and of all that it stands for in the national life. This is not, of course, to say that no building took place. On the contrary, anxiety for the fabric has been constant. But with the exception of the completion of the Towers in the 18th century no further addition has been made to the Church itself, and those who have been responsible for it have been concerned with preservation and, at times, with some not over-happy attempts at restoration. Curiously enough Westminster has never suffered from cracks or subsidences necessitating actual rebuilding. The problem has been to overcome the corroding effects of London's atmosphere on its external stonework. The result has been that the whole of the exterior has been so completely recased that practically none of the original external stonework remains.

Even in 1620 Dean Williams "found the Church in such decay that all that passed by, and loved the honour of God's house, shook their heads at the stones that dropped down from the pinnacles." He undertook extensive repairs on the North Front where the buttresses of the Nave "were almost crumbled to dust." But although, as his friend and biographer tells us, he used "durable materials" all his work had to be redone in succeeding centuries. None the less Williams has other claims on our gratitude. It was due to his love of music that Orlando Gibbons was appointed Organist at the Abbey. He made a "goodly Library" in the northern part of the former dormitory of the monks and furnished it with charming bookcases which still remain. Moreover he put up the chimney-piece of cedar wood with his arms upon it in the Jerusalem Chamber in order to commemorate the fact that he had entertained there the ambassadors who came over to arrange the marriage of Prince Charles with Henrietta Maria. It was unfortunate that his own fall from favour and the outbreak of the Civil War brought his activities at Westminster to a close.

The Civil War, in its early days, brought both destruction and desecration to the Abbey. Rovezzano's altar in Henry VII's Chapel together with the painted glass in the Chapel windows were destroyed, and some of the early 14th-century paintings on the Sedilia were mutilated no less wantonly. The Regalia together with the Royal vestments, which were kept at the Abbey, were removed to the Tower of London in order to be either broken up or sold. Peter Heylin, who was Sub Dean at the time, tells us that "the like ill fortune fell unto the Organs, Plate, Copes, Hangings, Altar-cloths, and many other costly utensils which belonged to the Church; all which were either broke in pieces, or seized upon and plundered for the use of the State." Desecration followed, for the soldiers were

Contra injuriam
Temporum
P
Guil: Bromley Ar:

Views of the Abbey Church before the time of Wren are rare, thus the engraving above, by Wenceslaus Hollar, dated 1654, is of especial interest. It shows the west end unfinished with the towers at only roof level. Against the North Transept is the Galilee Porch, built under Edward III about 1362 and destroyed in Charles II's reign. Below is an imaginative painting of the Abbey by William James, made between 1734 and 1740, to give an impression of the proposed additions to the Abbey which were never undertaken. A central lantern tower similar to the one outlined by Wren was suggested, and also two western spires in a mock Gothic style. The painting was made a few years before Hawksmoor actually added the towers we now know so well. Of particular interest is the representation of the houses which stood against the north walls of the Nave and east end of the Church.

quartered in the Church and "they not only brake down the Rails before the Table, and burnt them in the very place in the heats of July; but wretchedly prophaned the very Table itself, by setting about it with their Tobacco and Ale before them."

At the Restoration the Dean and the Prebendaries, who had been ejected during the Civil War and Commonwealth, returned to Westminster. It was not, however, until nearly forty years later than a serious attempt was made to deal with the extensive repairs which were then necessary for the fabric. In 1698 Sir Christopher Wren, who had been a boy at the School over fifty years before, was appointed Surveyor to the Fabric. Money was voted by Parliament and he at once undertook the complete refacing of the exterior on the south side. In a report which he wrote in 1713 he tells us that he found that the stone was decayed "four inches deep, and falls off perpetually in great scales." By that date a third of the necessary work on the exterior had been done and he was engaged on "the most dangerous part of the vaulting over the choir." In this work he used some of the stones from old St. Paul's, and the "painting upon Stone in imitacon of Sussex Marble" and the gilding of the ribs and bosses remain today as a memorial of his work.

Wren then proposed to add a steeple over the Lantern at the junction of the Transepts, which he felt sure had been meant to be part of the original 13th-century design. He himself had no great appreciation of Gothic architecture—the best he could find to say of Henry VII's Chapel was that it was "a nice embroidered work"—but he was too great a man not to realise that his proposed steeple should be "still in the Gothick form, and of a Style with the rest of the Structure" and "without any modern Mixtures to shew my own Inventions." In fact the steeple was never built, nor was Wren able to deal with the West Front before his death, although he saw that it was "very requisite to be finished," because the West Window was in a "crazy" state and "because the two Towers are not of equal Height, and too low for the Bells, which hang so much lower than the Roof, that they are not heard as far as they should be." Wren's work at Westminster has been much misunderstood. He is usually credited with the Western Towers, which, in fact, were begun in 1732, nine years after his death, and were the work of Hawksmoor and James. Wren was concerned mainly with the repair of the fabric, and it has been pointed out with some justice that "it is probably true to say that his careful and scientific treatment saved the Abbey at the time,"[1] although much of his work has had to be done again because the Oxfordshire stone which he used proved to be no more durable than the earlier stone from Caen and Reigate.

The Towers were building from 1732 to 1745, and in this period the great West Window was filled with painted glass by Joshua Price, probably from the designs of Sir James Thornhill who had certainly designed the glass for the Rose Window in the North Transept some few years before. The long story of repair

[1] *The Wren Society*, Vol. XI, p. 9.

THE ABBOT'S PEW

This panelled gallery of carved oak at the west end of the South Aisle of the Nave is known as the Abbot's Pew. It was built in the time of Abbot Islip in the early 16th century, together with rooms behind it including the Jericho Parlour (*see page* 48). Below it is a door giving access to the Church from these rooms. The central memorial is to the dramatist William Congreve, who died in 1729, much praised by his contemporaries, and who lay in state in the Jerusalem Chamber. Also standing in the Nave on the north side is the 16th-century oak pulpit (*below*). It is hexagonal in shape and has fine carved linenfold panelling on the side and on the standard which supports the sounding-board. Tradition has it that Archbishop Cranmer preached from this pulpit at the Coronation of Edward VI, the first Protestant king. At this part of the Abbey can be seen the distinctive break in the general uniform appearance of the Nave. To the left, or east, is the last bay finished in the late 13th century, with its richly diapered wall spaces, and to the right is the first bay of the work begun by Henry Yevele late in the 14th century. This part of the Nave is largely undecorated.

VAULTING BOSSES

Of recent years it has been possible to make a careful study of the bosses in the vaulting by means of photographic methods and many rewarding discoveries have been made. The bosses are of the most varied kinds and many of them exhibit a high standard of craftsmanship. The remarkable example left dates from the 13th century and is in the North Aisle of the Nave. It represents a man's head and shoulders, with an expression of agony on his face, surrounded by lions, two of which are tearing at his hair and two clawing at his breast. The exact significance of this magnificent piece of medieval art has yet to be explained.

and restoration has continued to the present day. It will be sufficient, however, to mention the heavy handed refacing of Henry VII's Chapel between 1807 and 1822, the necessary and often admirable work of Sir Gilbert Scott and the less satisfactory remodelling of the exterior of the North Front between 1875 and 1892.

The Little Cloister was part of the monastic Infirmary. Leading from the east walk of this delightful cloister are remains of the 12th-century Chapel of St. Katherine. Rooms built in the 14th century still stand to first-floor level all round the Little Cloister. These were built over in the late 17th century to provide houses for canons, but in 1941 many suffered heavily from fire in an air-raid. Those shown here have largely been rebuilt.

I have view'd and consider'd the Plann &
Elevation of the propos'd New Dormitory —
which is intended to be Erected in the
College Common-Orchard or Garden, and —
am of Opinion, That the Situation in —
That Place is much more Proper, and —
Convenient in all respects (for ye Lodging
of the Kings-Scholars) then the old —
Dormitory in Deans-Yard, or any other
Place contiguous to it, as will more fully
and plainly appear by the general Ground Flor
or Plann (made by Mr. Dickinson and —
lay'd before me for my perusal, to which
I refer.) Witness my hand this 20th day
of May, Ano. Dom: 1719.

Witness —
Chr. Wren
Ino: Tufnoll

Chr. Wren

THE WORK OF WREN

For over 20 years Sir Christopher Wren
was Surveyor to the Abbey, and in this
capacity he made a distinct impression on
the fabric. His principal work was the
entire refacing of the whole church with the
exception of Henry VII's Chapel. The stonework, then as now, was suffering severely
from the corrosive effects of coal smoke, and
in his restoration of the walls he removed the
external details of the original windows and
altered appreciably the great North Rose
Window. He designed several alternative
central lanterns, towers and spires but none
were built. Though often stated to be
Wren's own work, the upper parts of the
west front were actually carried out by his
pupil, Hawksmoor, after the master architect's death. He did make, however, a number of designs for a west front, and these are
still kept in the Abbey Muniments. He also
designed the New Dormitory for Westminster
School. The foundation stone was laid in
1722, but as Wren did not live to complete
the work the design was characteristically
corrected and "improved" by Hawksmoor.
Eventually Lord Burlington was called in,
and his dignified Palladian façade is at least
in accordance with the spirit of Wren's ideas.
On the left is a letter from Sir Christopher
Wren referring to the new School Dormitory,
and above is a view of the Abbey from the
old monastery garden. To the left is seen
the corner of Lord Burlington's Dormitory.

The "incomparable" CHAPTER HOUSE, one of the largest in England, was finished in 1253 and is of octagonal shape with a vaulted stone roof supported by a central pillar. The double entrance was restored in 1865 and a tympanum containing a Majesty added. On either side is an original Annunciation with censing angels. The surrounding walls are still largely covered with medieval paintings, and the floor is a rare example of 13th-century encaustic tile work. The windows were newly glazed in 1950. The beautiful interior was for three centuries concealed by galleries and presses containing the Public Records.

9

NEGLECT AND RESTORATION

THE completion of the Towers in 1745 was followed by a period, lasting roughly for a hundred years, during which those who had charge of the Abbey took little interest in the treasures under their care. Appreciation of Gothic architecture was at its lowest ebb. The fees which were collected for allowing every type of memorial and tablet to fill the Abbey seem to have been regarded as of more importance than any damage which might be caused to the fabric in attaching them to the walls. No restriction seems to have been made as to size for it was obvious that a large monument would mean a large fee. Nor does any question of the suitability of the monument to its setting ever seem to have been considered. The towering white marble monument to General Wolfe, if Horace Walpole had not intervened, would have displaced the 14th-century tomb of Aymer de Valence by the High Altar; it was only the weakness of the pavement which prevented the life-size statue of Addison, on its pedestal, from being placed in the Confessor's Chapel among the kings.

Many of the monuments themselves and the inscriptions on them could hardly be more inappropriate. The gallant admiral, Sir Cloudesley Shovell, appears reclining on a couch in full Roman armour with "a large perriwig with flowing curls"; an 18th-century Earl of Mountrath (until Dean Stanley discreetly removed him) was represented seated on a sofa in the clouds beckoning to his wife (slowly ascending with the help of an angel) to join him; Mrs. Mary Kendall, as her epitaph informs us, had many and great virtues and "these admirable Qualitys, in which she was equall'd by few of her sex, surpass'd by none, render'd her every way worthy of that close union and friendship, in which she liv'd with the Lady Catherine Jones."

These, of course, are extreme instances of foolishness and bathos. On the other hand it is only fair to say that many of these much-abused monuments have considerable merit, and by their very number and the variety of people whom they commemorate they add greatly to the interest of the Abbey and give it a representative character which would have been lacking in a church confined to the commemoration only of famous names. Those who clamour for their removal are not usually to be found among those whose appreciation of the Abbey is based upon knowledge of its history. It has been well said, and it is worth pondering, that "there is nowhere else in the world so long a range of monuments from the Shrine of the Confessor, the tombs of the Plantagenets, to the monuments of poets, and the more recent statues of statesmen, without any break— and all set in a framework so beautiful and so full of grandeur that, much as one may take exception to many of these works of monumental sculpture, they sink into insignificance in the building and do little or nothing to diminish the beauty of the whole."

On the whole the Abbey escaped lightly in the period under review. The worst schemes for "beautifying" it were never carried out. There were always a few who raised their voices in protest, and the only serious loss was the ruthless destruction of the original 13th-century choir stalls in 1775.

The turn of the tide may perhaps be marked by the publication in 1823 of Neale and Brayley's *History and Antiquities of the Abbey Church of St. Peter, Westminster*. This was an admirable piece of work, exactly describing the Abbey and everything within it at that date and written with knowledge and appreciation. It still remains an indispensable book. In 1849 Gilbert Scott was appointed Surveyor to the Abbey, and he held the post until his death in 1878. He was both competent and confident, and the work which he did at Westminster in preserving the fabric from further decay has hardly received the recognition which is its due. He was acutely sensitive to the beauty and interest of the Church under his charge, and if to a later age some of the things he did are open to criticism, he showed in his *Gleanings from Westminster Abbey* that he was the first man to study the Abbey in detail with real architectural knowledge.

His most outstanding work, apart from repair, was his restoration of the Chapter House from 1865 to 1873. This "incomparable" building, as Matthew Paris called it when it was built in 1250, after serving both as the Chapter House of the Monastery and as the meeting place of the Commons during the Middle Ages had been used from 1547 to 1863 as the depository for the Public Records. No care had been taken of the building, the original groining of the roof had been destroyed, the windows had been obstructed and mutilated and the whole of the interior had been cluttered up with galleries and presses containing the records. As Scott himself said he found "a noble work reduced to a wreck." He set out to restore it with delighted enthusiasm. In his *Gleanings* he describes how one day looking down behind one of the presses he saw "some round object in stone in the recess below. My curiosity being excited, I let down into it by a string a small bull's-eye lantern, when, to my extreme delight, I saw that the mysterious object was the head of a beautiful full-sized statue in a niche." It proved in fact to be one of the superb 13th-century Annunciation figures. Other discoveries followed such as the original tiled pavement, unrivalled elsewhere in England, which had fortunately been preserved by a wooden floor having been placed upon it, and the 14th-century paintings on the walls. Scott believed that he found warrant for everything which he did in restoring the building, and, although on

THE CENTRE OF
MONASTIC LIFE

In the Chapter House the day to day activity of the monastery was regulated. There the brethren would assemble after Mass to learn their tasks for the day, and after the novices had left the private business of the monastery would be discussed. Wrongdoers might be denounced and confessions made at the feet of the Abbot who would impose suitable penalties and punishment. This beautiful octagonal-shaped chamber had a further important function in the Middle Ages. From the reign of Edward I until 1547 it was one of the meeting places of the House of Commons, but the dual use ceased on the Dissolution and the Chapter House became Royal property which it has remained since.

The Chapter House is reached from the East Cloister Walk through the 13th-century vestibule. There is a flight of steps in the inner vestibule as the floor of the building is raised several feet above ground level to provide a crypt within the massive foundations. In it is a recess for an altar, and an aumbry and piscina. This crypt was one of the Abbey's treasure houses, reached only by way of a passage containing a pit-fall, and if a would-be marauder overcame this obstacle he would need to know the secret hiding places of the treasure within the 17 feet thick walls. The crypt nowadays serves as the Sacristy where the Abbey's vestments and ornaments of the altars are kept in presses and cupboards. In the soffit of the arch that contains the double entrance to the Chapter House are two rows of niches in a lacework of intertwined vines and foliage carved in stone. These hold small figures. On the sill at the side of the inner vestibule (*above*) stands a Roman sarcophagus, or stone coffin of oolite, on the front of which is a Latin inscription recording that the sons of Valerius Amandinus had it made in memory of their father. It is probably of 4th-century A.D. origin. On the lid is cut a cross which might be Saxon-work.

THE LADY
MARGARET BEAUFORT

The Lady Margaret Beaufort, the venerable mother of Henry VII, died in 1509 at the time of the Coronation of her grandson, Henry VIII. She was then staying in the Abbot's Lodging in the Precincts, and it is traditionally believed that two wooden trunks covered in red leather and bound with iron straps, now preserved in the Muniment Room, were the Lady Margaret's own chests. Both of these are used for storing, *inter alia*, the finely bound "indentures" (*see pages 70 and 71*) of instructions given by Henry VII to the monks concerning his new Chapel. Lady Margaret's name is inseparable from Abbey history. In her lifetime she was a great benefactress, a patroness of Caxton, and her tomb lies in the South Aisle of her son's new Chapel, while the Library now contains, by gift of the late Viscount Dillon, her "Book of Hours."

some points he was possibly mistaken, he did in fact restore the Chapter House in great measure to its former beauty.

In all his work at Westminster Scott found an enthusiastic supporter in Dean Stanley (1865–81). Stanley was fascinated by the historic associations of the Abbey. He knew little himself of architecture, he spent no time in deciphering original documents, but he was intensely interested in the lives and personalities of those commemorated within the Abbey, and he had read almost everything, however obscure, that had been written in prose or verse up to that time about the Abbey. With astonishing skill he gathered up all these threads and wove them into a brilliant tapestry in his *Memorials of Westminster Abbey* which remains a classic work of its kind.

Since the tall office and other buildings rose to the west and north in Victorian days, the conventional photograph of the Abbey has been of the Western Towers taken from a point in Victoria Street. With the demolition of the old Westminster Hospital, which stood a few yards north of the Western Towers, a new vista was opened. This photograph, taken from the roof of Central Hall, offers a view of the great church not seen for a century.

In a room at No. 20 Dean's Yard, formerly the Cellarer's House in the monastic establishment, are the early 16th-century wall paintings seen above. It is said that these were executed by Torrigiani's workmen when they were employed in Henry VII's Chapel. The signatures of almost the entire House of Windsor are seen (*left*) on the fly-leaf of a vellum copy of Ackerman's *Westminster Abbey* presented to the Dean and Chapter by King George V and his family. Below is an unusual view of the effigy of Maria, daughter of James I, who died in 1607 aged two. With her sister, Sophia, she lies in the "Innocent's Corner" of Henry VII's Chapel.

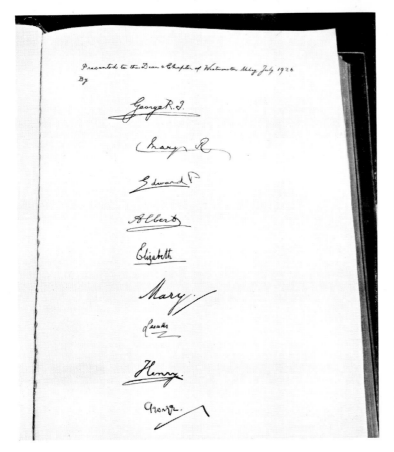

THE MOST HONOURABLE ORDER OF THE BATH

Apart from Coronations, Westminster is celebrated for two other Services in which the Sovereign and other Royal personages take prominent parts. One, the annual Maundy Service, is described on the facing page, while the other is the Investiture of Knights of the Most Honourable Order of the Bath.

This order of knighthood was founded in 1399 by Henry IV, and its name derives from the bathing ritual candidates were required to undergo to cleanse them of their sins. Knights were usually created at times of Coronations, and the ceremonies invariably took place in the Tower of London, where the Sovereign spent Coronation eve before proceeding to his crowning in the Abbey. After the symbolic washing, during which the King made the sign of the Cross on the bare backs of the knights, vigil was kept in St. John's Chapel. The next morning new members of the Order received their accolades before escorting the Sovereign on his progress through the City of London. Charles II was the last king to create Knights of the Bath in the Tower, and thereafter the Order fell into decay until revived as a military one by George I in 1725.

At this time, Henry VII's Chapel became the Chapel of the Order and the Dean of Westminster was made perpetual Dean of the Bath. Since then the provisions of the Order have been modified and extended several times, and now includes military and civil divisions. Only Knights Grand Cross, the senior degree, have stalls in the Chapel.

For the Service, the knights are splendidly robed in red mantles lined with white. The Sovereign, the Great Master, the Knights Grand Cross and the Officers of the Order assemble in the Chapter House with the Canons of Westminster and proceed into the Church to the Choir where a short Service is sung. Then the procession moves to Henry VII's Chapel for the elaborate ceremony of Investiture. The Sovereign makes an offering of gold and silver at the altar and presents his sword to the Dean who lays it on the altar to be redeemed by the Sovereign. The Great Master next delivers his sword and redeems it. Those Knights Grand Cross newly installed draw their swords and hold them hilt towards the altar, sheathing them again in unison with the Great Master. The ceremony in the Chapel being over the procession moves again to the Choir for the conclusion of the Service and finally returns to the Chapter House. Above is seen the procession for the 1951 Investiture moving through the Cloisters. Following the Dean is the Duke of Gloucester, the Great Master, and the Sovereign of the Order, His late Majesty King George VI.

THE MAUNDY SERVICE

Royal Maundy, the distribution of alms and (at one time) the washing of feet of the poor on the Thursday of Holy Week, has been regularly performed since the reign of Edward I. The name derives from the *mandatum* of Our Lord to love one another, and to this day the opening words of the Service are "A new Commandment have I given unto you. . . ." From the early 16th century as many old men and as many old women as there are years in the Sovereign's age have received the gift. The Maundy is distributed in traditional red, white and green leather bags. In one are as many Maundy pennies as the Sovereign has years, in another a pound in lieu of the redemption of the Sovereign's gown, with money in lieu of provisions (once given), and in the third is an allowance for clothing. The specially minted silver Maundy money now comprises penny, twopenny, threepenny and fourpenny pieces; the recipients are generally former rate-paying and tax-paying householders. In 1932, for the first time since the time of James II, King George V distributed his Maundy in person, and since then the Sovereign has frequently taken part in the Service. Above is a photograph of Queen Elizabeth II leaving the Abbey on Maundy Thursday, 1952, after carrying out the first public engagement of her reign. Her Majesty is escorted by the Dean and the Lord High Almoner.

On the left is the tomb of the Unknown Warrior in the Nave. On Armistice Day, 11th November, 1920, the body of an unknown soldier, disinterred at random from the hosts of British dead in France, was re-buried in the presence of King George V and "a vast concourse of the nation." Flanders poppies—emblems of sacrifice—always decorate the tomb.

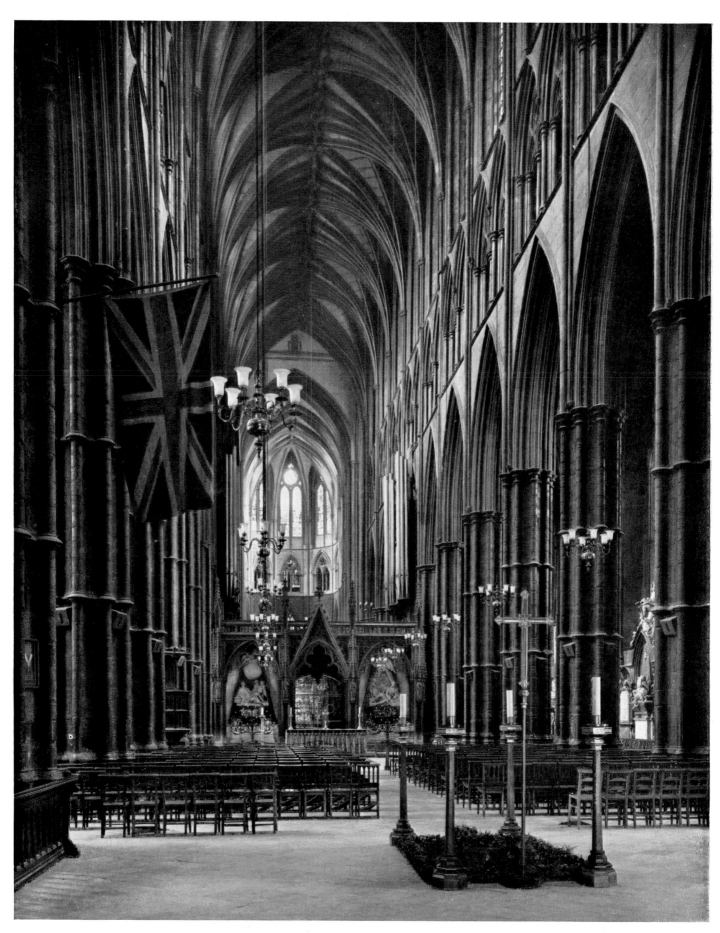

THE NAVE. A view of the whole length of the Abbey Church from west to east gives a fine impression of its proportions. High above the flowing arches the great sexpartite stone vault rises, springing from the slender wall shafts. Separating the Nave from the Choir beyond, stands the choir screen and organ loft. In the foreground is the tomb of the Unknown Warrior. The Padre's Flag, the bloodstained Union Jack used as altar cloth and funeral pall at the Ypres Salient, and which draped the coffin when the Unknown Warrior was buried here on 11th November, 1920, hangs above the Tomb. Below on the column is preserved the medal presented by the American Congress and laid by General Pershing beside King George V's Wreath one year later.

10

RECENT WORK AND DISCOVERIES

HE present century has seen another and a great advance in our knowledge of the Abbey. Stanley's successor, Dean Bradley (1881–1902) appointed Dr. E. J. L. Scott to explore the hitherto almost unknown treasures of the Muniment Room, although this vast collection of documents exceeded in number those possessed by any cathedral or church in England. With patient and unselfish labour Dr. Scott worked for a quarter of a century at cataloguing the collection, and gradually he brought order out of chaos. On the foundation thus laid Dean Armitage Robinson (1902–11), Dr. E. Pearce, the Revd. H. F. Westlake and others were able to base their studies of monastic life at Westminster and thus add greatly to our knowledge of that period of the Abbey's history. And this is only one corner of a vast field of documentary history which is being, and still has to be, explored.

In 1906 and 1925 Professor W. R. Lethaby, who had been appointed the Abbey Surveyor in 1906, published his two books on the Abbey.[1] These books not only broke new ground but they revolutionised the whole study of the Abbey. For the first time the names of the Master Masons and craftsmen who built and adorned the Abbey were rescued from oblivion, and their work at Westminster was brought into relation with their work elsewhere. Moreover the whole fabric of the Church and its contents were minutely studied and re-studied with profound knowledge and sensitive appreciation. No detail escaped Lethaby. He felt that "from its crowded associations, and the many lovely minor works it contains, as well as its own intrinsic beauty, this church must be held by Englishmen as the supreme work of art in the world," and to him every stone which it contained was sacrosanct.

The repair of the exterior of the North Front (1872–92), under Scott and Pearson was, it may be hoped, the last of the restorations on what may be called "Early English" lines. Although much care and architectural scholarship was expended upon it, when at length the scaffolding was removed it was but too clear that the uninspiring façade which was disclosed was merely a careful reproduction of what it was believed the original façade must have looked like, complete with new statues and carving, while all that had remained up to that time of original

---

[1] *Westminster Abbey and the King's Craftsmen* (1906) and *Westminster Abbey Re-examined* (1925).

work had disappeared in the process. Such a reconstruction would have been impossible under Lethaby. The keynote of the work undertaken by himself and his successors has been repair and preservation and not reconstruction.

Above all there has been undertaken the systematic cleaning of the interior stonework of the Abbey. The result has been rewarding beyond anyone's hopes. The work is slow and laborious, and it had to be discontinued during the last war, but it has been an unending delight to see Henry VII's Chapel, the South Transept and part of the Apse emerging clean and fresh almost as it left the hands of the original builders. It has been no less a pleasure to cleanse and "discover" the almost inexhaustible things of beauty which the Abbey contains. No one who has not seen it at close quarters can have any idea of the dirt and grime which still blurs and almost hides much of the original sculpture and the bosses in the roof. To take but one example of many. A few years ago there was in St. Faith's Chapel a 13th-century corbel head which from the ground looked a black and shapeless mass. When it was cleaned there emerged a head—the "dreaming youth" as it has been called—of such beauty that it is now numbered among the supreme things which the Abbey contains.

Other discoveries have been made too. The existence of the extensive foundations of the Norman Abbey just beneath the floor of the Nave was quite unsuspected until they were revealed by chance in 1930. Equally unexpected was the discovery of the mural paintings in the South Transept to which reference has been made in an earlier chapter. One further discovery may be mentioned partly because of its interesting sequel.

Shortly before the Second World War the monument of an Elizabethan Dean was being cleaned in St. Benedict's Chapel. The Dean is represented kneeling at a prayer-desk. On removing this desk it was found that it had concealed a little square window in the wall behind. It had long been a puzzle why there was a blocked door in the wall beyond, which seemed to have had no very obvious purpose. It was then remembered that among the Abbey Muniments there were records that the Abbey Anchorite or Recluse, who was usually an elderly monk living a life of contemplation in a cell of his own, had given from time to time offerings to the Altar of St. Benedict. It seemed likely, therefore, that what had been found was the previously unknown site of the Anchorite's cell with its window looking into the Chapel. If so, it must have been through the now blocked door that the young Richard II passed to consult the Anchorite before going out to meet Wat Tyler, and also Henry V when he spent the night of his Accession with the Anchorite and vowed to reform his life.

This was an interesting discovery, but, perhaps, even more interesting was its apparent confirmation. A month or two afterwards, a curious reference was found in the autobiography [1] of a certain Thomas Raymond who, it would seem, in 1629 was living with his uncle, Sir William Boswell, in what he describes as a "little straight house built in a corner . . . as soon as you are out of the east door

---

[1] *Autobiography of Thomas Raymond*, Camden Society, 3rd Series, Vol. XXVII, pp. 26–27.

THE WEST END. This great arch of the South West Tower is a noble piece of 15th-century work. It encloses St. George's or the Warriors' Chapel, which in 1932 was dedicated to commemorate the dead of the First World War. On the column outside hangs the great contemporary portrait of Richard II, presented to the Abbey by that King, and described on page 39.

of Westminster Abbey," that is to say roughly on the site of the suggested cell. He tells us that his Uncle was sometimes laughed at for the humbleness of his lodging, but that he used to justify it by telling the following delightful story[1] with, for us, its dramatic conclusion;—

"In the latter times of Henry VII, a prebendary,[2] of this Church (having lived most of his life in his cloister coming little in the world) was persuaded by some friends to go to a masque at Court where he hardly ever had been, but never saw such a sight, the masques very glorious and the King and Court in mighty gallantry. The masque ended not till well towards morning, and the prebendary returned home hugely satisfied and admiring the glories he had seen, and rose not that morning till towards ten of the clock. And being very still, these things much possessed his thoughts, and, having received many civilities at the masque from several great courtiers, he resolved to go to Court to return them thanks and again to feed his eyes with the glories there.

And coming to the Court, the great Gates were both open and no porters attending, and passing farther the yards were strewed with straw; not a creature to be seen. Going up stairs in the like case to the Guard Chamber, there he found only bare walls, dust and rubbish, and the tables and trestles thrown about. Then to the Presence Chamber where he had seen the Cloth of State, rich hangings, yet nothing but dust and bare walls, and one corner a poor old man with a piece of candle in his hands—the Court being that day removed—looking for pins.

This so sudden and strange a change from what he had with admiration seen the night before struck such a serious consideration into him of the mutability of the glories of this world that, returning to his monastery, he within a while after bound himself an anchorite. And in this very place where our lodging now is was his cell, having a little hole through the Church wall, by which he could see the high altar and hear mass. Where he in great devotion lived and died."

The lodging has been pulled down long since, but it was extraordinarily interesting to find the suggestion that in all probability the Anchorite's cell was on this site apparently confirmed, even to the "little hole" looking into the Church, by one who was reporting what was evidently still a living tradition at the time that he wrote.

It has seemed worthwhile to set this story out at length as giving some indication of the kind of work which has been carried out at the Abbey within recent years. It shows, too, the inexhaustible interest and fascination of this great Church which it is the privilege of those who are connected with it to preserve, to cherish and to reverence.

[1] The spelling has been modernised.
[2] *sic*. He meant, of course, a monk.

THE GREAT LITLYNGTON MISSAL

The great illuminated manuscript volume known as the Litlyngton Missal, executed in 1383–84, when Nicholas Litlyngton was Abbot, is unique. It is twenty inches long by thirteen and a half inches wide and stands above all other works of its day in the sumptuousness of its decoration, the elegance of its writing and the delicacy of its miniatures. The Missal was the Service Book for the High Altar, and it contains not only the daily offices of the Abbey but also those necessary in a Royal church, where by long tradition, Coronations and Royal funerals were held. With the smaller Liber Regalis (*see page* 47) the Missal provides posterity with the form of ritual used at Coronations in the 14th and 15th centuries. Preserved in the Abbey Muniments is the original account for the making of the book: the cost was £34 13s. 7d., the scribe was Thomas Preston. The text is in black ink with the rubrics in red, and most of the pages have fine borders of patterned panels overflowing with foliage and flowers. The opening of each principal office or service is adorned with a miniature similar to those of the Coronation of a king (*below, left*) and of a queen consort (*below, right*). The most striking illustration of all is the full-page representation (*right*) of the Crucifixion superbly decorated in gold, blue, green, vermilion and fawn.

THE DECAYING FABRIC

The Abbey was originally built of Reigate stone, and in subsequent restorations Portland and Bath stones were used. In the formation of these stones calcium carbonate binds the particles together. The action, however, of sulphuric acid generated in the London atmosphere, chiefly by coal fires, on the calcium carbonate causes the stone to disintegrate. In such manner serious damage has been wrought among the pinnacles, flying buttresses and the stages of the upper walls. The process of decomposition is hastened by acid soot deposited on the surface; delicate carved details such as finials and crockets are particularly affected in this way. The photograph (*bottom, right*) shows the result of corrosion on a parapet. This damage is not easily visible from the ground, but what can be seen are dark stains which indicate that the stones are in varying stages of decomposition. At first a blistered crust forms on the surface, decay sets in and the stone falls to dust (*below*). At an advanced stage the masonry is rotten throughout, joints fail and the structure becomes insecure (*bottom, left*). In the Cloisters the damage caused by lack of protection from wind and moisture may be seen at close quarters: the Dean (*left*) stands by a badly eroded column. This destruction can and must be arrested. Towards saving and then maintaining the fabric, the Dean and Chapter have launched their £1,000,000 Appeal Fund.

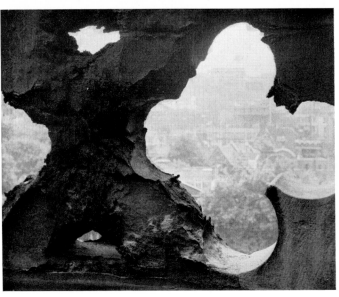

The Embossed Communion Plate dates from 1681. The candlesticks, slightly later in origin, were bought with the legacy of Sarah Hughes, housekeeper to one of the Prebendaries. The Altar Cloth was given by King George V and Queen Mary at their Coronation.

II

THE ABBEY TREASURES

By Canon Adam Fox, D.D., Archdeacon of Westminster

THERE is a law of life which is expressed in the words: "To him that hath shall be given." Henry III after building so fine a church as Westminster Abbey might have guessed that it would receive many handsome additions and adornments. And so it has been. The greatest of these, because it is so large and so beautiful, is Henry VII's Chapel; but the great Plantagenet tombs, including Henry III's, are splendid too, and more a part of the original church. From these, through every gradation of carven tomb and altar, we come to the smaller things, the plate and the hangings which adorn the altars, and more secular items such as books and manuscripts.

As Treasurer of Westminster Abbey I am mainly concerned with the very necessary and very exacting duty of "making both ends meet." But I have also a somewhat indefinite responsibility for "The Treasures," and my first care in this matter must be to determine what is and what is not "a treasure." I think myself entitled to hand over to the care of the Surveyor of the Fabric all those monuments and memorials which could not possibly be removed without tools and tackle. But there remain many things which could be picked up and carried away, if no one was looking, and which often have to be carried about by authorised persons. A good number of them were in part transferred to St. James's Palace for a public exhibition in January 1953.

Such things the Treasurer is ultimately responsible for in some sort of way, and so in my mind they count as the Abbey Treasures. One of the striking and perhaps unexpected things about them is to find how few of them are very old. The old altar-plate, furniture, hangings and other adornments which were movable, disappeared in Cromwell's time. We have no medieval treasures of this kind except the so-called Retable. Our earliest piece of plate is dated 1571 and did not come to us till 1918. But the new altar-plate, which was procured in the latter part of the 16th century, is very fine, and the candlesticks for the High Altar (1691) are superb. So are the copes used at the Coronation (1661) and the Funeral (1685) of Charles II.

But many of our things have not belonged to us for as long as sixty years. This is true of all the altar-crosses and nearly all the altar-clothes. Up to the end of the last century the Abbey must have been one of the drabbest of the large churches in England. Today the frontals for the altars and the copes for the ministers form a very fine collection of modern work, much of it connected with recent Coronations. On the other hand we have not in modern times surpassed or even matched the Charles II copes. But the truth is that the Abbey has constantly inspired munificence, and where benefactors of any period have given the best then available, that best is very good indeed.

ABOVE: The Hearse Cloth, given by the Actors' Church Union in 1920 in memory of the members of the theatrical profession who fell in the first World War, is of white silk brocade with embroidered arms and badges. It was first used in connection with the burial of the Unknown Warrior in the Abbey, and was lent for the Lying-in-State of King George V, and of Queen Mary in Westminster Hall. On it rests a sword—Henry V's own weapon, according to tradition, and believed to have been used at his funeral. BELOW: All the Abbey altar-plate was destroyed during the Commonwealth. These plain silver-gilt chalices and flagons were the first replacements after the Restoration. The Alms Dishes, nineteen inches across, are hall-marked 1684–85.

A RARE MADONNA

RIGHT: The Virgin and Child by the Venetian painter Bartolomeo Vivarini (*c.* 1480). It was presented to the Abbey by Lord Lee of Fareham in 1935 as an altar-piece for Henry VII's Chapel. BELOW, *left*: One of 95 statuettes set in niches beneath the clerestory windows in Henry VII's Chapel. These represent a great variety of saints and scholars; this one is of St. Matthew. He carries a book because he wrote a Gospel; he wears spectacles because (so it is said) he had ruined his eyesight while engaged as a tax-gatherer. He was thus occupied when he was called to be an Apostle. The statuettes are thought to be Flemish. BELOW, *right*: A detail from the so-called Retable—the original decoration which stood above the High Altar. It is eleven feet long and three feet high, and was once used as part of a waxwork case. Although painfully damaged, enough remains to show that the Retable was highly ornamented with glass and gilt gesso enclosing a number of superb paintings. This work is undoubtedly of 13th-century date; the detail shown here is from the Raising of Jairus's daughter.

99

ABOVE: An Altar Piece, depicting the Madonna and Child with Saints and Angels, by the Florentine painter Bicci di Lorenzo (1373–1452). It was bequeathed by Lord Lee of Fareham, and hangs normally on the south side of the Sanctuary. Behind it is a 16th-century Brussels tapestry. BELOW, *left*: Two of the three copes of crimson velvet embroidered with gold and silver thread, made for the Coronation of Charles II. The cope on the right was worn by the Dean at Queen Elizabeth II's Coronation. BELOW, *right*: A cope of gold thread possibly made from the Coronation Robe of Charles II. The cloth is likely to have been woven in Italy though the pattern is Chinese. The cope is a fine piece in fairly good condition but too fragile to be worn.

THE CROSSES

TOP, *left*: The Cross of Westminster, which leads the processions in the Abbey, was presented by the Hon. Rodman Wanamaker of New York as a symbol of brotherly union and concord between the United States and Great Britain. It is fashioned of ivory, silver-gilt and gold, and is the work of Messrs. Barkentin and Kraal. TOP, *right*: The Cross of Ivory is carried in front of the Dean. It was made from one of two elephant tusks presented to the Abbey by Haile Selassie, Emperor of Abyssinia, as a thanksgiving for the restoration of his country, 1944. RIGHT: The chairs and faldstools for the use of King George VI and Queen Elizabeth were given in 1949 by the Canada Club as a memorial to Canadians who fell in the second World War. They were designed by Mr. Sebastian Comper, and are made of Canadian wood ornamented with gilt metal. The fine and large carpet on which the chairs stand was given some years previously by prominent Canadians resident in London.

THE EDWARD VII VESTMENTS

TOP: On the occasion of the Coronation of King Edward VII a great quantity of handsome stamped crimson velvet was provided. Here we see the altar frontal and three of the nine copes made of this material ornamented with gold thread to the design of Mr. J. T. Micklethwaite, and also the dorsal at the back of the altar ornamented with badges and crowns to the design of Lord Mottistone. These vestments are still in constant use. The Altar Cross was given by the 5th Earl of Rosebery when his daughter was married to the Marquess of Crewe in 1899.
RIGHT: The two alms-dishes presented by the Queen, then the Princess Elizabeth, and the Duke of Edinburgh on the occasion of their marriage in the Abbey in November 1947. Notice the reflection in the left-hand alms-dish of a king embroidered on an adjacent dorsal.

THE R.A.F. CHAPEL ORNAMENTS

ABOVE: The Cross and Candlesticks of pale silver-gilt made for the Royal Air Force Memorial Chapel in 1947 by Mr. Seymour Lindsay in conjunction with Professor E. A. Richardson. The design is of Renaissance character. The great height of the Cross in relation to the size of the Chapel—more often known as The Battle of Britain Chapel—gives an impression of great dignity. A large spherical crystal unites the Cross to its stem. TOP, *left*: An Elizabethan patten and chalice, said to have been recovered from the bed of the river at Oxford. The patten acts as a cover. This, the oldest Communion plate possessed by the Abbey, is dated 1571; the ornamental band round the chalice is characteristic of the period. The chalice has only been in the keeping of the Dean and Chapter since 1918, when it was given in memory of a young officer, Lieutenant Cyril Dude, who fell in battle on 21st March in that year. LEFT: A silver Cross of Abyssinian workmanship on an English stem. It was given at the end of June 1902, when the Coronation of King Edward VII was postponed owing to his illness. The Abyssinian Envoy to the Coronation, Ras Makunan, asked the Dean's permission to make a "votive offering to Westminster Abbey, coupled with his own fervent prayers, for the restoration to health of the stricken monarch." This Cross was the offering he made. Its unusual shape and the delicate but irregular pierced silver work make it most attractive.

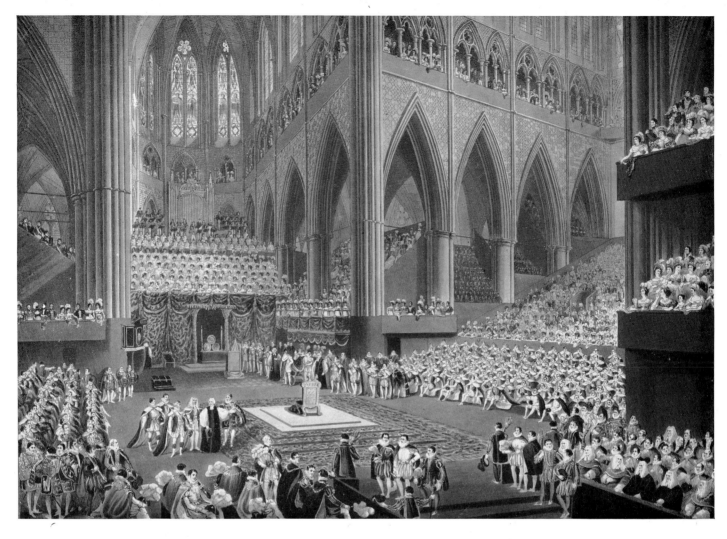

CROWNING PLACE OF KINGS

By the time Henry III commenced to pull down King Edward's Church to make way for his own glorious creation, Westminster was firmly established as the place of Coronation. His architect, Henry of Reyns, therefore, deliberately adopted an unorthodox feature of the original Church by placing the Choir west of the central crossing. As will be seen from the plan on page 16, a deep space between the Choir and the steps leading to the Sanctuary and High Altar was thus provided; and it is within this space—technically termed the Theatre—that for 700 years the Sovereign has been crowned. In medieval times, in the centre of the space, a "mount" or "scaffold" about six feet high was erected and upon this King Edward's Chair stood. It is now the practice to raise the level of the Theatre floor to the height of the Sanctuary steps, King Edward's Chair being placed between the High Altar and the Throne which stands on a separate dais. On the right is seen the layout of the Theatre as arranged for the Coronation of Queen Elizabeth II; the reproduction of the print above—of the Recognition rite at the Coronation of George IV—gives a fair impression of its spaciousness.

It will be seen from the plan that the arrangement of the Theatre for the last Coronation was precisely the same as for George IV's crowning except in points of detail. In fact since the 17th century the appearance of the Theatre has altered hardly at all. The seating arrangements for the great congregation are also very similar from one Coronation to the next, though at each successive ceremony the need to provide more seats in the Abbey has increased until in 1953, with tier after tier rising almost to the vault in the Nave and Transepts, the limit of accommodation—for some 7,500 guests—was reached.

The Earl Marshal bears the responsibility for making the necessary material arrangements in the Abbey for a Coronation, and the building operations are carried out by the Ministry of Works. When they are complete the Dean and Chapter hand the keys of the Abbey to the Earl Marshal for security reasons.

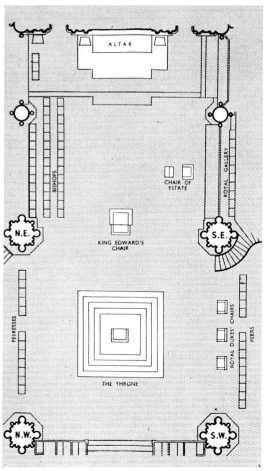

The Annexe built for the Coronation of H.M. Queen Elizabeth II. It was designed by the Chief Architect's Division of the Ministry of Works under Mr. Eric Bedford, A.R.I.B.A.; the wash drawing is by Mr. Terry Pledge, also of the Ministry of Works.

12

THE CORONATION OF QUEEN ELIZABETH II

BECAUSE the Sovereign is crowned at Westminster no book purporting to tell the story of the Abbey would be complete without the subject of the Coronation being included. In *The History of the Coronation**— a companion to this volume— the origins of the Service from the earliest times have already been traced and an informative introduction to the Coronation of Queen Elizabeth II provided. The history is now taken further by the presentation of a continuous pictorial record of Her Majesty's hallowing on 2nd June, 1953. This record is preceded by a photograph of the splendid setting of the solemn Service of dedication and consecration in order that something may be conveyed of the transformation the interior of the Abbey undergoes before a Coronation can take place. It will be seen by comparing this photograph with those which appear earlier in this book that the change in appearance is considerable. For several months the Church is closed to the public while a forest of scaffolding rises and the monuments are boarded up. From the West Door to the Choir, a broad carpeted procession-way is flanked by tiered galleries, and from the floor to the great Rose Windows and the clerestory in both transepts rise many rows of seats. For Queen Elizabeth II's crowning a blue-and-gold motif was adopted. The carpet from the West Door to the Choir was in two tones of dark blue, that which covered the great

space of the Theatre being of golden colour. The hangings of the galleries were of a lighter shade of blue relieved by national and Commonwealth emblems in gold.

The exterior appearance of the Abbey is also altered for a Coronation. At the west end a large covered area has to be provided wherein the Procession can be marshalled before proceeding into the Nave. This temporary structure, known as the Annexe, follows contemporary architectural taste; the design for the 1953 Coronation is reproduced above. Beneath the cupula was the entrance through which the Queen and the principal guests entered the Church. Between the pillars of the cupula an enormous Royal coat of arms was suspended; flanking the vast expanse of window stood statues of heraldic beasts; above them were national, Dominion and Colonial emblems. Within the Annexe were robing and retiring rooms for the Queen, the Duke of Edinburgh and the Royal Family, and for the peers and peeresses who took part in the Procession.

Such then was the setting for the thirty-eighth Coronation at Westminster since the Norman Conquest, the thirtieth in the present Church. Her Majesty came to the Abbey of Kings as her ancestors had done before her, and a further magnificent scene was added to the great panorama upon which for nearly a thousand years the momentous events of the Realm have been recorded.

* By Lawrence E. Tanner.

The Abbey as arranged for the Coronation of Queen Elizabeth II seen from a viewpoint above St. Edward's Chapel. In the foreground is the Theatre with King Edward's Chair and the Throne on its raised dais. The Queen's Chair of Estate and faldstool is placed in front of the Royal Gallery which may be identified by the adornment of gold altar plate. Above the Royal Gallery Her Majesty's personal guests and the Royal Household were accommodated; the Bishops occupied the three rows of chairs seen bottom right of the photograph. Facing the Throne, between the great piers, are the chairs for the Dukes of Edinburgh, Gloucester and Kent; behind the Royal Dukes in the South Transept, as customary, were the peers and in the North Transept, the peeresses. In the Choir Stalls were the places of the Prime Ministers of the Commonwealth, the Government of the United Kingdom, Royal and other foreign representatives; above them to the left the galleries in the Muniment Room held Privy Councillors, civil servants, and high ranking officers of the three armed forces of the Crown.

For a Coronation, the State Regalia is brought from the Tower of London on the day before the Ceremony and is placed in the custody of the Dean of Westminster. Overnight the jewels rest in Jerusalem Chamber guarded by Yeoman Warders from the Tower, and early on Coronation morning they are carried in procession by the Dean and Canons of Westminster to the positions at which they will be needed during the ritual. To the singing of the Litany, the Regalia procession moves from the Chamber through the Cloisters and into the Church to the High Altar, then into St. Edward's Chapel, finally reaching the Annexe. Above, the Dean is seen bearing St. Edward's Crown; below, the Prebendaries are portrayed with other articles of Regalia.

Queen Elizabeth II was the fifth Sovereign of the United Kingdom to be crowned from Buckingham Palace. Above is seen the State Coach leaving the forecourt on the morning of 2nd June, 1953, before proceeding to Westminster by way of the Mall, Trafalgar Square, the Embankment and Parliament Square. Her Majesty was accompanied by the Duke of Edinburgh wearing the full dress uniform of Admiral of the Fleet. Five other Queens Regnant had come to the Abbey before her for their Coronations but of them all none was a more beautiful or a more radiant Queen as is evident from the photographs below.

THE ENTRANCE INTO THE CHURCH: Since the Coronation of Richard I in 1189 it has been customary for the clergy to lead the Grand Procession into the Abbey Church, the Sovereign preceded by the Regalia being the last to enter. In the photograph above, the Queen having passed into the Nave is approaching the Organ Loft. As Her Majesty emerged from beneath it, she was greeted by the shouts of the Queen's Scholars of Westminster School—VIVAT REGINA ELIZABETHA! VIVAT! VIVAT! VIVAT!—the privilege of first acclaiming the Sovereign by age-long tradition being that of the Westminster boys.

THE RECOGNITION

This, the first act of ritual, is a survival from the past for it preserves the ancient form of the people's ratification of the election of the Sovereign. It may be likened to " banns of marriage," for in theory, opportunity is afforded for dissent. Immediately after the Anthem the Archbishop accompanied by the Great Officers of State, Garter King of Arms preceding them, went first to the east side of the Theatre, then to the south, west and north sides in turn, and at each presented the Queen to the people. Her Majesty meanwhile stood in full view, facing each side as the Archbishop spoke : *Sirs, I present unto you Queen Elizabeth your undoubted Queen : Wherefore all you who come this day to do your homage and service, Are you willing to do the same ?* The people's shouted reply of GOD SAVE QUEEN ELIZABETH was followed by the sounding of trumpets. On the left the Queen, supported by her Bishops, the Bishop of Durham on her right and the Bishop of Bath and Wells on her left, the train of her robe of crimson velvet borne by her six train bearers, has entered the Theatre and is about to be seated in her Chair of Estate on the south side. Above is the splendid scene as, having made her private prayers at the faldstool before her Chair, the Queen awaits the commencement of the Recognition ritual.

THE OATH: By her answers to a series of questions the Queen promised to govern her peoples according to the laws of the land and to uphold the Protestant Faith. Kneeling at the High Altar Her Majesty laid her right hand on the Bible saying: *The things I have here before promised I will perform and keep. So help me God.* She then kissed the Book and signed the Oath (above). In the succeeding act of ritual, THE PRESENTING OF THE HOLY BIBLE, the Moderator of the General Assembly of the Church of Scotland took part in the Coronation Ceremony for the first time, receiving the Bible from the Dean and speaking the words: *Here is Wisdom; This is the Royal Law; These are the lively Oracles of God* as he made the presentation (below).

THE ANOINTING : This is the most sacred and mystical part of the Coronation Service. In one sense the Anointing sets the Sovereign apart from the people by investing her with spiritual authority, while in another it makes her the consecrated head of the Commonwealth. It is because of the deep spiritual significance of the ritual that the actual anointing of the Sovereign with Holy Oil on the palms of the hands, on the breast, and on the crown of the head is hidden from view by a Canopy of cloth of gold. The Anointing rite commenced with the Queen kneeling at her faldstool before her Chair of Estate. The Archbishop began the hymn VENI CREATOR SPIRITUS which was followed by a short prayer and the anthem " Zadok the Priest " that has been sung at this point of the Service for nearly 1200

years. Meanwhile the Queen, having completed her devotions, was disrobed of her crimson robe, and invested with a plain white linen garment, and being seated in King Edward's Chair, the Canopy of cloth of gold supported by four Knights of the Garter was brought and held over her. From the historic Ampulla, the Dean of Westminster poured the Holy Oil into the Anointing Spoon and with this the Archbishop administered the unction to Her Majesty . . . *As Solomon was anointed King by Zadok the priest and Nathan the prophet, so be thou anointed, blessed, and consecrated Queen over the Peoples, whom the Lord thy God hath given thee to rule and govern.* After the Blessing the Queen was divested of her plain white garment and invested with the *Colobium Sindonis* and the Supertunica or Close Pall of cloth of gold.

PRESENTING THE SPURS AND SWORD

The golden Spurs were brought from the Altar and presented to the Queen. Her Majesty touched them, thereby recognising chivalry and all that chivalry implies. The presentation of the Sword followed. The bearer of the Sword of State delivered it to the Lord Chamberlain, and in its place received from him the Jewelled Sword. This was delivered to the Archbishop who laid it upon the Altar. Then, after a short prayer, the Archbishop placed the Sword in the Queen's hands and as Her Majesty held it (above) he exhorted her : . . . *With this sword do justice, stop the growth of iniquity, protect the holy Church of God, help and defend widows and orphans, restore the things that have gone to decay, maintain the things that are restored* . . . Then the Queen rising from King Edward's Chair (right) offered the Sword to the Altar, wherefrom the Lord who first received it redeemed the bejewelled symbol by paying its traditional value, one hundred shillings.

THE DELIVERY OF THE ORB: This act of ritual was preceeded by the Investing with the Armills, the Stole Royal and the Robe Royal. The Orb, symbol of independent Sovereignty under the Cross, was brought from the Altar by the Dean of Westminster and delivered into the Queen's right hand by the Archbishop who said: *Receive this Orb set under the Cross,* *and remember that the whole world is subject to the Power and Empire of Christ our Redeemer.* To enable Her Majesty to receive the Ring of kingly dignity, the Glove, the Royal Sceptre, ensign of kingly power and justice, and Rod of equity and mercy in the immediately succeeding ritual, the Orb was then delivered by her to the Dean of Westminster to be laid by him upon the Altar.

THE PUTTING ON OF THE CROWN

The Crowning is the climax of the Coronation Service, the supreme moment to which the whole process of Investiture leads. The ritual commenced with the people rising from their seats and the Archbishop standing before the Altar. His Grace took St. Edward's Crown into his hands and laying it again on the Altar before him made a short prayer : *O God, the Crown of the faithful : Bless we beseech thee this crown and so sanctify thy servant ELIZABETH upon whose head this day thou dost place it for a sign of Royal Majesty, that she may be filled by thine abundant grace with all princely virtues : through the King eternal Jesus Christ our Lord.*

Then the Archbishop, assisted by the other bishops, came from the Altar to King Edward's Chair in which the Queen was seated. From the Dean of Westminster, the Archbishop received the Crown and holding it above the Queen's head in a superbly timed pause lowered it reverently (above and below left). At that precise moment the people cried GOD SAVE THE QUEEN repeatedly and loudly, and the princes and princesses, the peers and the peeresses put on their coronets and caps, the trumpets sounded and the guns at the Tower thundered their salutes. As the acclamation ceased the Archbishop continued : *God crown you with a crown of glory and righteousness, that having a right faith and manifold fruit of good works, you may obtain the crown of an everlasting Kingdom by the gift of Him whose kingdom endureth forever.* The Queen having received all the ensigns of Royalty the Archbishop pronounced the Benediction (above).

This magnificent photograph captures the spiritual emotion and drama of the scene in the Abbey immediately before the Queen was crowned. As the Archbishop poised St. Edward's Crown above Her Majesty the peers and peeresses and the Kings of Arms prepared to put on their coronets and make their acclamation. History, once again at Westminster, was about to be repeated.

THE ENTHRONING: Symbolically, it is by this act of ritual that the Sovereign enters into and takes possession of the Kingdom. Rising from King Edward's Chair, the Queen, crowned, sceptred, and wearing the Robe Royal, turned to the west and accompanied by the Archbishop, her supporting Bishops, the Great Officers of State and the Lords bearing the Regalia, proceeded to the raised Throne. Above is the scene as this movement took place. The Great Officers of State, the Lord Chancellor and the Lords who bore the Regalia are grouped around the Throne, to the right of and before which stand the Archbishops of Canterbury and York, and the attendant bishops. The Queen approaches the Throne; standing by the great column are the Lord Mayor of London, Garter King of Arms and other officers of the College of Arms and of the Lyon Court. On the extreme right of the photograph is the Duke of Edinburgh, and in the Royal Gallery, to the left of the column, may be seen Queen Elizabeth the Queen Mother with the Duke of Cornwall, who, although under five years old, was brought to the Abbey for the latter part of the Service, the Princess Margaret, the Princess Royal, and the Duchesses of Gloucester and Kent.

THE ENTHRONING: Having reached the Throne, the Queen was lifted into it by the Archbishops and Bishops and when the attendant Lords had assumed their positions on the dais the Archbishop said: *Stand firm, and hold fast from henceforth the seat and state of royal and imperial dignity, which is this day delivered unto you, in the Name and by the Authority of Almighty God, and by the hands of us the Bishops and servants of God, though unworthy. And the Lord God Almighty, whose ministers we are, and the stewards of his mysteries, establish your Throne in righteousness, that it may stand fast for evermore.* The photographs above and right were taken as the Archbishop made this Exhortation.

A new Throne is provided for every Coronation. Queen Elizabeth II's Throne was of 17th-century design made of carved English lime and beech woods, gilded with English gold leaf and covered in hand-woven silk crimson damask. The Royal Cypher enclosed in the Garter and surmounted by St. Edward's Crown was richly embroidered in blue and gold silks on the front and back.

THE FEALTY OF THE BISHOPS

The Sovereign having been Anointed and Crowned and Enthroned before the people, could now receive the Homage of the princes and of the spiritual and temporal peers. After Her Majesty had delivered the two Sceptres to the Lords who had carried them in the Procession a small cushion was placed at her feet (right). The Archbishops and Bishops make their act of Homage first because the lands for which in ancient days they paid fealty were held in the name of the Church. The spiritual peers therefore do Homage as the first estate of the Realm and not as holders of baronies, and as such take precedence of the temporal peers. Thus as head of the Church of England the Archbishop of Canterbury began the Homage (below). Ascending the steps of the Throne he, with the Supporting Bishops, knelt before Her Majesty and, placing his hand between hers, promised : *I Geoffrey, Archbishop of Canterbury, will be faithful and true, and faith and truth will bear unto you, Our Sovereign Lady, Queen of this Realm and Defender of the Faith, and unto your heirs and successors according to law. So help me God.* He then kissed the Queen's right hand. As the Archbishop paid his fealty the rest of the bishops knelt in their places and spoke the words of fealty simultaneously. Before 1902, all peers, spiritual and temporal, made their homage personally but at the Coronation of Edward VII, with the view of shortening the Ceremony, the precedent was set that only the senior peer of each degree should kneel before the Sovereign and this has been followed since.

TEMPORAL HOMAGE:
HOLY COMMUNION

Immediately after the spiritual peers, the Duke of Edinburgh made his Homage. His Royal Highness ascended the steps of the Throne (above), and having taken off his coronet, knelt before the Queen and, with his hands held between hers, spoke the words: *I Philip, do become your liege man of life and limb, and of earthly worship; and faith and truth I will bear unto you, to live and die, against all manner of folks. So help me God.* Arising, he touched the Crown on the Queen's head and kissed her cheek. The Homage of the Duke of Edinburgh was followed by that of the Dukes of Gloucester and Kent who in turn were followed by the senior peer of each degree.

After the Homage came the celebration of Holy Communion. The Queen descended from the Throne and having been divested of her Crown and Sceptres offered Bread and Wine which the Archbishop reverently placed upon the Altar. The Queen next made her Oblation, offering an Altar Cloth and an Ingot of gold before being united in the Sacrament with her Consort, who, coming from his chair, removed his coronet and knelt beside Her Majesty (right).

In St. Edward's Chapel, during the RECESS, the Queen was disrobed of the Robe Royal by the Mistress of the Robes assisted by the Lord Great Chamberlain and the Groom of the Robes and arrayed in her Purple Robe of State. Then, supported by her Bishops and wearing the Imperial State Crown and carrying the Sceptre of the Cross in her right hand and the Orb in her left hand and preceded by the Great Officers of State, Her Majesty took her place in the Procession. This meanwhile had formed in the Theatre before proceeding to the West Door. Above, the Queen is seen passing the Throne and the Princes of the Blood Royal, the Duke of Edinburgh already having left his Chair and taken his place in the Procession through the Church.

The superb and solemn scene in the Nave as the Queen approached the West Door. The procession way is lined by Yeomen of the Queen's Bodyguard, officers of the Honourable Company of Gentlemen-at-Arms flank the Procession. Immediately behind the Queen's train bearers is the Mistress of the Robes who in turn is followed by the Groom of the Robes.

Above is seen the entrance to the Annexe with its modernistic cupula and immense Royal coat of arms. On the extreme right is the archway which leads to Dean's Yard and the Cloisters. The Queen and the Duke of Edinburgh have just entered the State Coach drawn by eight Windsor greys in gilded and crimson harness for the State Drive through London. Postillions in gold-braided red jackets and jockey caps are astride the near side horses, walking men are at the head of each horse and grooms attend the Coach. The Earl Marshal, having escorted the Sovereign from the Abbey, stands by a pillar of the cupula.

THE STATE PROCESSION

In medieval times, the Sovereign, usually bareheaded, showed himself to his people during the Procession from the Tower of London to Westminster on Coronation eve. This custom was abandoned after the crowning of Charles II. Up to the Coronation of George IV, the great banquet in Westminster Hall followed the Abbey Ceremony and completed the celebrations, but when this also was abandoned it became the custom for the Sovereign to drive in State through London before returning to Buckingham Palace. On the left the Queen is seen leaving the Annexe for the State Procession. She still wears the Imperial State Crown and carries the Sceptre with the Cross and the Orb and, thus invested, was seen by over a million of her subjects along the five-mile-long route. Her Majesty is about to step into the State Coach which is seen in all its magnificent golden detail below. It was built for George III and completed in 1762 at a cost of over £7,500. From four carved tritons the coach is slung; eight members representing palm trees support the roof which is surmounted by three cherubs bearing the Imperial Crown. The front, side and rear panels carry allegorical scenes painted by Cipriani, and the rear wheels, nearly six feet in diameter, follow the design of those of an ancient triumphal car. All four wheels are now rubber-shod.

The boys of the Westminster Abbey Choir School in the Cloisters where their predecessors once practised and played their games.

THE ABBEY MUSIC AND CHORISTERS

Not the least of the glories of the Abbey is the music. This has long been so. Whilst other churches might be content with what is good, Westminster has always sought choral perfection. Through the centuries the magnificent solemnities of Coronations and Royal marriages, *Te Deums* for victories of arms, and masses for the passing of souls have been sung with transcending beauty, and it has thus become traditional for Westminster to excel at music. Orlando Gibbons, Purcell, John Blow and William Croft all served as organists, and all lie buried in Musicians' Aisle; and some of the greatest church music now heard at services throughout the world was composed for the Abbey. Henry Purcell in particular did much to maintain Westminster's pre-eminence in ecclesiastical music. He was born in 1658 in St. Anne's Lane near the Abbey, becoming organist at the age of twenty-two. During his short life Purcell arranged and composed the music for many state ceremonials including the Coronation of William and Mary, and of Queen Anne. He died in 1695 and was buried in the Abbey "in a very magnificent manner," the anthem which he composed for Mary II's funeral being sung at his interment.

The early history of the Westminster choristers is lost in obscurity, but it is probable that boys joined the novices and monks in the singing of masses as far back as 1170. In 1479 there was a master of singing boys, in addition to the master of the grammar boys, and there is a record of the names of the choristers for 1511–12. The foundations of Henry VIII and Elizabeth I provided for the education of choristers with the forty scholars of Westminster School. In 1846 a separate choir school was set up in a room at the King's Arms in nearby Bowling Street, and later the first boarding school for choristers was established in Little Smith Street.

There is now a choir school for thirty-six boys drawn from every social class and from every part of the country. About six boys are selected each year, the main qualification being, in addition to a suitable voice, that of a Christian background. Parents who cannot afford the very low school fees are assisted from Chapter funds. The present boarding school is in Dean's Yard, and here the tradition of perfection is maintained but without sacrifice of the boys' general education as so often was the case in the not very distant past. The Organist of the Abbey is responsible for choral instruction; a headmaster and his staff provide a normal preparatory school education which fits the boys to enter public or state-aided grammar schools.

The men of the Abbey Choir are known as lay vicars and there are twelve of them—four for each voice. They, too, are part of the Elizabethan foundation, and like their predecessors for four centuries, they are professionals.

In modern times for Coronations and other great State services the Abbey choir is joined by the choirs of the Chapels Royal, and representatives from St. George's Chapel, Windsor, St. Paul's Cathedral and other choirs, and is accompanied by an orchestra of about sixty players.

125

ACKNOWLEDGMENTS

The publishers wish to express their appreciation of the wholehearted co-operation of the Dean and Chapter of Westminster in the production of this book. Permission was given for Mr. Harold White to work in the Abbey during the greater part of the summer and autumn of 1952 and for a colour reproduction to be made of the Canaletto painting of the Western Towers for the frontispiece. Apart from the Dean, who kindly consented to write the Foreword, other members of the Collegiate Church made notable contributions. The publishers are grateful to Canon Adam Fox for his descriptions of the Abbey Treasures; to Mr. E. W. Thompson, Headmaster of the Choir School, for help with the article on page 125; to Mr. T. Hebron, C.B.E., M.V.O., Registrar, for invaluable advice; to Mr. J. W. Franklin, Assistant Librarian, for writing most of the captions, and to Mr. J. G. O'Neilly, Assistant to the Surveyor, for guidance in regard to the fabric and for the plan of the Abbey. The photographers are acknowledged on the facing page, but it should be mentioned that the Dean's Verger, Mr. G. C. Drake, M.V.O., and his staff rendered great assistance to Mr. Harold White whilst he was working in the Abbey. The kindness of Canon Charles Smyth, Rector of St. Margaret's, Westminster, in allowing the wall paintings in No. 20 Dean's Yard to be photographed is also acknowledged.

All the half-tone engravings in this book and the colour plates for the frontispiece were made by W. F. Sedgwick, Ltd., photographic engravers to His late Majesty King George V. It should be mentioned that the press photographs of the Coronation of Her Majesty Queen Elizabeth II were taken under extremely difficult conditions and that the engravings, perforce, had to be made at great speed.

Publisher's Postscript

The earlier pages of this book and the dust-jacket were printed before Mr. Lawrence E. Tanner's advancement in the Royal Victorian Order from Member to Commander was made known in the Coronation Honours List.

BIBLIOGRAPHY

The following are among the principal works consulted:

Henderson, A. E.: *Westminster Abbey Then and Now*, 1937.

Lethaby, W. R.: *Westminster Abbey and the King's Craftsmen*, 1906.

   ,,   ,,   *Westminster Abbey Re-examined*, 1925.

Perkins, Dr. Jocelyn: *Westminster Abbey; its Worship and Ornaments* (3 Vols.), 1938.

Scott, G. G.: *Gleanings from Westminster Abbey* (2nd edition), 1863.

Stanley, A. P.: *Memorials of Westminster Abbey* (5th and final edition), 1882.

Tanner, L. E., and R. P. Howgrave-Graham: *Unknown Westminster Abbey* (A King Penguin book), 1948.

Westlake, H. F.: *Westminster Abbey* (2 Vols.), 1923.

Royal Commission on Historical Monuments; an Inventory of Westminster Abbey, 1924.

Westminster Abbey Muniments.

THE PHOTOGRAPHS

The majority of the photographs that illustrate this book were taken by Mr. Harold White, F.I.B.P., F.R.P.S., who was commissioned by the publishers to make an exhaustive photographic survey of Westminster Abbey. Mr. White worked in the Abbey for several months confining himself generally to broad vistas and to the Abbey Treasures. For the close-up studies of architectural details, for the documents from the Muniments and for some of the effigies, the publishers are indebted to Mr. R. P. Howgrave-Graham, F.S.A., Assistant Keeper of the Muniments who, in the many years he has been associated with Westminster, has built up a collection of more than 1,000 photographs of his own taking. It should be mentioned that many of Mr. Howgrave-Graham's studies, especially those of bosses, corbels and similar small sculptures high in the walls and the vault, were made when staging erected for cleaning and restoration work was available. Mr. Howgrave-Graham took full opportunity of these rare occasions, and the photographs he made are at the same time unique, beautiful and of great architectural and historical interest.

CECIL BEATON   frontispiece, H.M. Queen Elizabeth II.

HAROLD WHITE, F.I.B.P., F.R.P.S.   Pages: 4, 6, 7, 8 *top*, 11, 13, 14, 15, 18, 21, 23 *top right and bottom left*, 25 *top right*, 26 27, 28 *top right and left*, 31 *top*, 33, 35, 37 *top right*, 38 *top left and bottom right*, 39 *top left*, 40, 43, 45 *top right*, 46, 48 *top and bottom right*, 51 *top right*, 53, 56, 57 *top and bottom right*, 58 *top right and bottom left*, 61, 64 *top*, 67 *top and bottom right*, 69 *top right*, 72 *bottom right*, 73, 79 *top right and bottom left*, 80, 81 *top*, 82, 85 *top*, 87 *top*, 89 *bottom*, 90, 93, 96 *top left*, 97, 98, 99 *top right and bottom left*, 100 101, 102, 103, the back jacket illustration.

R. P. HOWGRAVE-GRAHAM, F.S.A.   24, 25 *top and bottom left*, 31 *bottom left and right*, 37 *top, centre and bottom left*, 38 *bottom left*, 45 *bottom left*, 47 *top right and bottom left*, 48 *bottom left*, 50, 51 *top and bottom left*, 54, 55 *centre and bottom left*, 57 *top left*, 58 *top left*, 63, 64 *bottom left and right*, 69 *bottom left*, 70, 71, 72 *top and centre*, 74, 79 *bottom right*, 81 *bottom*, 85 *bottom*, 87 *bottom right*, 95, 96 *bottom left, top and bottom right*

PETER PARKINSON   the front jacket illustration.

WARBURG INSTITUTE   28 *bottom right*, 39 *bottom right*, 45 *top left*, 99 *bottom right*.

TOPICAL PRESS   47 *top left*, 67 *bottom left*, 86, 113 *top*, 114, 115, *bottom right*.

BRITISH MUSEUM   8 *bottom*, 23 *bottom right*.

CENTRAL PRESS   55 *top right*, 87 *bottom left*.

WESTMINSTER ABBEY   77.

KEYSTONE   88.

P.A. REUTER   89 *top*, 119 *top*.

ILLUSTRATED   125.

MINISTRY OF WORKS   105.

PRESS PHOTO COMBINE   106, 108 *bottom left*, 109, 110 *top*, 111, 112, 115 *top right*, 116, 117, 118 *top*, 119 *bottom*, 120, 121, 122.

KEMSLEY PHOTO SERVICE   107 *bottom left*, 110 *bottom*, 113 *bottom*, 115 *top left*, 118 *bottom*, 124.

SPORT AND GENERAL   107 *top*.

B.I.P.P.A.   107 *bottom right*, 123.

PHOTOGRAPHIC NEWS AGENCIES   108 *top and bottom right*.

INDEX

THE HISTORY & TREASURES OF WESTMINSTER ABBEY

BY LAWR   ., V.P.S.A.